# RETURN TO SHIVA

*Seek this wisdom by doing service, by strong search, by questions, and by humility; the wise who see the truth will communicate it unto thee, and knowing which thou shalt never fall into error.*

SHRI KRISHNA

# SACRED TEXTS

## GENERAL EDITOR

## RAGHAVAN IYER

This series of fresh renderings of sacred texts from the world's chief religions is an inspiring testament to the universality of the human spirit. Each text is accompanied by an instructive essay as an aid to reflection. In the ancient world, before the proliferation of print, seekers of wisdom thought it a great privilege to learn a text, and sought oral instruction from a Teacher in the quest for enlightenment. The scriptures of all traditions are guides to the attainment of serene continuity of consciousness through the practice of self-study, self-transcendence and self-regeneration in daily life.

# SACRED TEXTS

THE DIAMOND SUTRA (with selections from Buddhist literature)

RETURN TO SHIVA (from the *Yoga Vasishtha Maharamayana*)

THE GATHAS OF ZARATHUSTRA (Zoroastrian texts)

TAO TE CHING by Lao Tzu

THE GOLDEN VERSES OF PYTHAGORAS
    (with the commentary of Hierocles)

IN THE BEGINNING (from the *Zohar*)

THE GOSPEL ACCORDING TO THOMAS

THE SEALS OF WISDOM (from the *Fusus al-Hikam*) by Ibn al-'Arabi

# RETURN TO SHIVA

*Return to Shiva* is a fresh rendering of eighteen selections from the *Yoga Vasishtha Maharamayana*. Composed by the Rishi (Seer) Valmiki, it contains the perennial quintessence of the Hindu spiritual tradition. Cosmology, psychology and a refined mode of living are presented in terms of higher states of consciousness. The texts translated here focus on Shiva, the archetypal *Guru* or spiritual Initiator and the supreme regenerative force in the cosmos. The book includes an instructive essay, "Jnana Yoga", by Raghavan Iyer and concludes with Shankaracharya's "Ten-Versed Hymn" and a glossary of terms.

# RETURN TO SHIVA

## FROM THE YOGA VASISHTHA
## MAHARAMAYANA

### RISHI VALMIKI

CONCORD GROVE PRESS
1983

**CONCORD GROVE PRESS**
*London    Santa Barbara    New York*

First Printing: August 12, 1983

ISBN 0-88695-006-6

# CONTENTS

4

*This exhaustless doctrine of Yoga I formerly taught unto Vivaswat; Vivaswat communicated it to Manu and Manu made it known unto Ikshwaku; and being thus transmitted from one unto another it was studied by the Rajarshees, until at length in the course of time the mighty art was lost, O harasser of thy foes! It is even the same exhaustless, secret, eternal doctrine I have communicated unto thee because thou art my devotee and my friend.*

SRI KRISHNA

AUM

# JNANA YAGNA

Osiris, Krishna, Buddha, Christ, will be shown as different means for one and the same royal highway of final bliss—Nirvana. Mystical Christianity teaches *self*-redemption through one's own seventh principle, the liberated Paramatma, called by the one Christ, by the others Buddha; this is equivalent to regeneration, or rebirth in spirit, and it therefore expounds just the same truth as the Nirvana of Buddhism. All of us have to get rid of our own Ego, the illusory, apparent self, to recognise our true Self, in a transcendental divine life.

THE MAHA CHOHAN

*Mind is the sacrificer, and the upward-life is the fruit*
*of the sacrifice. For it brings the sacrificer day by day to*
*the Eternal.*

PRASHNA UPANISHAD

During the primeval dawn of human evolution, the whole of humanity was suffused with a spontaneous devotion to Gurus and Preceptors. Simultaneously, all found no pain but a pure pleasure in the performance of the daily duties of life, revealing an intimate connection between devotion and duty. The conception of such a humanity differs totally from our own. It is like a Golden Age far removed from our time, because for many centuries we have engendered, with extraordinary violence and pertinacity, the falsehood of a separate identity for each human being, supposedly gestated at birth and terminated at death. People tend not to think about death and live as if they have a kind of invulnerability. But they blunder through without any knowledge of who they are, and find themselves oppressed by a sense of inward confusion, which only allows them to speak and think in terms of comparison and contrast. They are driven by their dwarfed conceptions of success and failure and are trapped in differentiated consciousness based on unending comparison and contrast. At the same time, this consciousness assumes an apparent stability not intrinsic to it, but involving a shutting out of the archetypal moments of birth and death. In time, this means forgetfulness, an indifference to the primary facts that apply to all humanity — that there is a great continuity to the human pilgrimage, that death is followed by rebirth, that this is true not only for particular souls but also that there is a continuous passage from generation to generation. The whole process is so vast that the moment we try to limit it, in terms of crude conceptions of duty or obligation, we also feel that any personal devotion we show is gratuitous. Captivated by personal differentiated consciousness, we live under the sway of the specious idea that the universe is for one's own private benefit and that each one is favouring the world, favouring other human beings, by an egocentric stance, by supererogatory acts, and that if one is devoted one has set up some kind of claim upon the object of devotion.

All of this thinking is distorted, inverted, and perverted, bound up with the descent of consciousness into matter. At a certain point of material density and fragmentation of consciousness, the pale reflection of the unmanifest light of the Immortal Triad assumes a false centrality. This would be like a shift from the self-luminous centre of a circle to a lit-up region which only seems luminous by contrast with the shadow around. The latter is the spurious ego, the limited personal consciousness. Given this condition, every human being can, at one level, understand that there is something very beautiful and elevating, something extremely authentic, in poetic accounts of a Golden Age of primordial humanity, when human beings moved naturally and related to each other beautifully. They were spontaneously held together by an effortless sense of moral and spiritual solidarity with the whole of nature, with those before and those yet to come, and above all, with their great Teachers. Though we can resonate with such an Age, we also know that if we have to ask questions about it, we already presuppose that it is estranged from us.

What good, then, can come of talking about devotion for a person who has become totally convinced that he has no capacity for any feeling, any devotion for anyone else? Who is that person? A cerebral machine, chatting away, insecure, confused yet making judgements? Is that the whole of that person? But if he has assumed this is all he or anyone else is, how can talking about devotion make a difference? Suppose such a person were told that there are great beings like Shiva, Krishna and the Buddha, hosts of hierophants seated in meditation and constantly engaged in ideation upon universal good, who have so vast a perspective of endless time, boundless space and ceaseless motion, that they can see the rises and falls of civilizations and epochs in perspective. Suppose he were told that they can see the antics of human beings in much smaller spans of time and space with unwavering compassion, and also that they can see the root illusion. These beings are involved in universal welfare and uplifting the whole of humanity. Any human being who can vibrate in mind, heart and self to the tune of the great universal impulse of these mighty beings, may serve as a focal point through whom some mitigation of human misery and some elevation of consciousness is possible.

To the sick, as in the time of Jesus, the idea of a super-healthy human being does not speak. Similarly, how can a person completely incapable of ordinary feelings grasp the idea of such noble beings? Unconsciously that person has been ceaselessly worshipping at the altar of the material self — and not even doing a very good job at it, not even being constant in devotion to his own personal self — inattentive, afraid, fickle, confused. With the lunar shadow as his only focus, how can such a person comprehend the light of the Spiritual Sun? How can such a person grasp the perspective of Mahatmas? But then, even if the person cannot comprehend those beyond him, can he still apprehend something that is at once universal and archetypal, which is found throughout the animal kingdom in the love and protection shown by animals for the young, which is found in the human kingdom between mothers and children? Even with all the corruption of modern modes and relationships, we still find this pulse of decency, warmth and kindness, a dauntless trust that is in the human heart. Surely a person should be able to reawaken that which now has been buried and obscured but which was once strong and secure.

This is the point at which a person can benefit from the teaching of *Jnana Yajna* — Wisdom-Sacrifice. Lord Krishna came at a time when he knew that humanity could not go back and restore its child-state without any effort. But on the other hand, he also knew that human beings were going to be enormously vulnerable to self-righteous merchants of the moral language who narrow and limit conceptions of duty and morality by institutionalizing them, and thereby bind human beings through fear to mere externalities of conduct. Therefore an alternative had to be shown. Being magnificently generous, Krishna speaks at the widest cosmic level of how the Logos functions out of only a small portion of itself and yet remains totally uninvolved. It is like the boundless ocean on the surface of which there are many ships, and in which there are many aquatic creatures, though the depths of that boundless ocean remain still. The whole world may be seen from the standpoint of the Logos, which is essentially incapable of incarnating and manifesting within the limitations of differentiated matter. The Logos can only overbrood. This overbrooding is joyous, producing myriad kaleidoscopic reflections within which various creatures get caught. Krishna gives the great standpoint, the divine perspective, which is all sacrifice. That is the critical relationship between the unmanifest and the manifest, because if the unmanifest can never be fully manifested, how can the manifest ever be linked to the unmanifest? There is always in everything that is manifest, behind the form, behind the façade, a deathless core of the very same nature and of the very same essence as that which is unmanifest. Where a human being can, by the power of thought, bring this to the centre of individual consciousness, it is possible to consecrate. It is possible to act as if each day corresponds to the Day of an entire universe, or to a lifetime. It is possible to act in each relationship as if it were a supreme expression of the very highest relationships between teacher and pupil or mother and child. It is possible to act in a small space as if there is the possibility of an architecture and rearrangement which can have analogues to the grand arrangements of solar systems and galaxies.

This is the great gift of creative, constructive imagination without illusion. What makes it Wisdom-Sacrifice is that one trains personal consciousness — the chattering mind, the divided and wandering heart, the restless hands — one centres all of these energies around a single pivotal idea, having no expectations. If an ordinary human being had no expectations whatsoever, the person would die simply because typically a person lives on the basis of some confused and vague expectations in regard to tomorrow, next year and the future. Deny a human being all expectations, all claims and personal consciousness usually will collapse. Of course this cannot be done from the outside. The shock would be too great. But human beings can administer the medicine to themselves progressively and gradually. Merely look at the years already lived and see how many expectations have been built up. Either you dare not look back at them and how they were falsified — which means there is a cowardliness, a lie in your very soul — or you have replaced them so fast by other expectations that you are caught in a web of externalizing expectations. To initiate a breakthrough you can earnestly think, "Supposing I have only one day more to live; supposing everything that I have is taken away from me; supposing I can rely on nothing and expect nothing. What would be the meaning of joy, the dignity of grief?''

If a person then thinks of Shiva or Krishna, of the unthanked Mahatmas and Adepts, and thinks of them not as distant from the human scene but as the ever-present causal force behind the shadow play of history, then he finds an incredible strength in that thought, a strength in consciousness but without a solidification of the object of consciousness. One can act with a freedom that is ultimately rooted in total actionlessness, like the supreme light of the Atman which is in eternal motion but which is not involved in what we call motion, refracted by differentiated matter. At the same time, one can live as if each act is supremely important, sublimely sacred. The person who really comes to think this out trains himself in this mode of thinking, feeling, breathing, acting and living and can in time gain a new lightness and economy, a fresh conception of true necessity, but above all a fundamental conception of identity — merely as one of manifold unseen and unknown instruments of the one Logos.

This is the great teaching of *Jnana Yajna* which, stated in this way, looks difficult, but is at the same time at some level accessible to each. It is a teaching so sacred that it is veiled in the *Gita* — hidden when it is given in the fourth chapter and again at the very end of the eighteenth chapter. It is a teaching which, if fully grasped, is the gateway to freedom and will enable one to become karmaless, to avoid becoming caught through the mind in the intertwining chains of karma. Clearly, karmalessness was not possible for early humanity, but it had all the ingredients of the quality which must belong to the mature person of the present when adopting the standpoint of those pioneers of the future who act self-consciously with a universal perspective and without residue, without becoming involved in the externalities or, as Gaudapada taught, without leaving any footprints.

The difficulty of this can be appreciated when we recall that in the fourth chapter of the *Gita* Krishna says that there are some who sacrifice the in-breathing and the out-breathing, while others chant the texts, and still others actually surrender themselves. All these sacrifices arise out of action. They arise out of the non-self and retain the illusion of an agent. In every one of these sacrifices we can distinguish archetypally five elements. There is that which is the oblation offered in sacrifice. There is the fire into which it is offered. There is the instrument — a ladle or whatever — with the help of which the offering is placed in the fire. Then there is the agent, the 'I', the person who says, "I am performing the sacrifice." There is the object of the sacrifice. All of these exist at one level in a universe of differentiated matter, constituted of innumerable beings that are ever at work and interacting in ceaseless motion. There is the interplay of subject and object, the deceptive contrast between light and shadow. There are separate objects and a background. All of this is maya, the projective yet veiling power of the Logos, of the Ishwara, of Krishna.

A human being does not have to project or be taken in by the veiling. It is possible for him to stand apart from roles, from sounds and sights, and to see through and beyond the seeming separation of objects. To take a simple example, we have artificial light, and by it we see and focus. We see many colours, a room, separate people. If we turn all the lights off, some people will be uncomfortable. Suddenly we no more see objects, selves, colours, contrasts, but we can then experience the breathing and pulsation of human beings. Paradoxically, we would have a greater sense of what it is to be human when all lights are turned off, when we can sense the collective breath of so many human beings, than when in an illuminated room we see faces, contrasts, colours, and all the differentia of the external plane.

This is true of every archetypal mode of sacrifice rooted in action. It is mayavic. Wisdom-Sacrifice begins with the recognition that all of these are mere epiphenomena, only appearances cast upon the one *Brahman*, the ever-expansive, immeasurable force, essence, spirit, primordial matter — call it what you will because no distinctions apply at that level. That boundless existence, *Brahman*, the Supreme Spirit, is the offering; *Brahman* is the fire; *Brahman* is the mode of making the offering; *Brahman* is each of us and the person making the offering; *Brahman* is the object of the sacrifice. If *Brahman* is *all* these, why become focussed upon specific differentia?

We all have experience of this when we witness a noble piece of music performed by a superb orchestra, or when we watch a moving play with the most highly synchronized and dedicated actors. As Shakespeare said, "The play's the thing." There is a sense of something beyond all the details, the incidents, the scenery and the individual actors. There is an intricate interplay that points beyond itself. But we try to reconstruct — and that often happens, alas, because it is one of the futile tendencies of human beings — instead of keeping very quiet and assimilating a deep experience in music or in drama. We are tempted to share it with someone else, and in the telling, we distort, fragment and emphasize contrasts. When one gets to the extreme condition of those congenital critics who are compelled to do this habitually, a sad destruction takes place. The person who does this propagates a distortion. His life is truly "a tale told by an idiot, full of sound and fury, signifying nothing." How much did such a human being add to the sum-total of good when he breathed his last? What difference did his life make to other human lives, to the relief of human pain, to the liberation of human minds, to the enlightenment of human hearts?

We have to recover the sense of the transcendental, unmanifest One. We have to reach again and again to that which is above the head, that which is without any parts or attributes, that light which can never be mirrored except in Buddhi, the only part of a human being that is capable of mirroring Atman. Buddhi is usually mostly latent, but if Buddhi mirrors Atman there is an infallible result, a decisiveness and assurance which nothing else can give. *Nischaya* is the word in Sanskrit, meaning 'without any shadow'. When a person, in the depths of meditation, out of the very finest ineffable feeling, touches that pure vessel of the Atman in the inmost brain, a perfect mirror of the colourless omnipresent light, there arises an assurance and certainty which is constant and can never be destroyed. Equally, it can never be shared or verbalized though it becomes the constant, central fact of life. This is irreversible. Even though a person has made many mistakes over many years — wasted words, harsh sounds, violent speech, empty words — even though a great deal of karma has been generated, all of which will have to be rendered in full account in future lives, nevertheless, if one truly touches the inmost core of the soundless sound and achieves that supreme sense of decisiveness, clarity, confidence, and calm, then it is possible to negate and counteract a lot of the karma produced in the past.

Wisdom-Sacrifice is the mode of creative speech in silence,

meditating upon the soundless sound, where there is no attachment, no involvement, and one does not participate in lesser emanations. The Pythagorean Monad, like the human triad, emanates out of the total darkness, initiating a universe, and withdraws forever after into the darkness. Human beings can initiate in that spirit, can come out of the vast silence of contemplation to begin something and let a whole series follow while withdrawing totally. They thus exemplify the archetypal stance of the Mahatmas. The very fact that we can think about such ideas, understand and appreciate them, means there is that in us which, though fearful of death, is willing to cooperate now with the consciousness which after death will witness the separation of the principles, and take stock of a lifetime to prepare itself for the karma of the future. It is possible to cooperate in waking life with that perception which, in deep sleep, represents an unbroken, undivided consciousness. Then there is no limitation of space, time or energy in one's perspective and understanding of humanity and the universal good, and one can insert oneself into the whole.

Anyone who can, as a result of deep meditation, start with small beginnings and try to utter a word to help or heal another human being, or who can stay in a period of silence for the sake of some larger purpose of benefit to humanity, can come to know what it is to initiate. To gain the power of the Initiator, one must both specialize and concentrate magnetism and be attentive enough to apply a thought with such controlled precision and perfect timing to the needs of another human being that one can make a permanent change for the good in that person's life. In the light of Wisdom-Sacrifice, *Jnana Yajna*, good and bad are merely relative appellations from the standpoint of differentiated consciousness in time and space. We grow over a lifetime in making finer and finer discriminations because the cruder relativities with which we live prevent us from understanding a great deal of human life. If this is true of the world around us, it is also true of ourselves.

This has been put in the form of a story about the three *gunas* — *sattva*, *rajas* and *tamas* — all of whom are compared to impostors who accost a man in the jungle. We are told that *tamas* is the one who assaults the victim for the immediate purpose of robbery, *rajas* is the one who binds him up for the purpose of making the proper kill, and *sattva* is the one who releases the person, can take him to the edge of the forest but cannot go any further. *Sattva* is afraid of what is outside the forest. He is also a thief, but his theft is through goodness. It is an attempted theft of that illimitable light of the spirit which can never be captured or translated into attributes.

A person must see all his limitations and weaknesses as shadows of certain qualities which are the painstaking results of karmic good works in previous lives, but which still are bonds, because they become ways in which one defines oneself. *Sattva* involves one as a personal self in imagining that one is better than others, that one is separate from the beast and the most wretched. It is fundamentally unable to rise to the level of the compassion of Shiva, Krishna and Buddha, who can see in all the same diffused light throughout the great masquerade of maya, but who also perceives the many degrees of enslavement to the masquerade which can only be overcome during a long period of time. Krishna says to Arjuna that though he is grieving for all these people, they are better off gone. They cannot in their present incarnation emancipate themselves from their lifelong qualities, but they can in the future. In an unlimited universe there is hope for all, but in any limited period of time everybody cannot progress equally or to the same extent. To understand this is common sense. It is part of the mathematics of the universe. But to use that understanding with wisdom and compassion means we must not become excited about beginnings and endings or about when and where such and such happened to whom. We must not be caught up in all of this because this is the very framework that binds, especially when it is cloaked in one's better qualities. The light of the *prajnagarbha* – the Atman beyond and above all the *gunas* and qualities — is a wisdom that is essentially unmanifest and is the perpetual motion which is pure motionless self-existence.

We need to say to the personal conditioned self, "Even though you are incapable of appreciating the grandeur of the cosmic sacrifice, I, that Self which knows that you are incapable, take you and throw you into the cosmic fire." Now this can be treated ironically but it is also profoundly sacred. It is what H.P.Blavatsky termed 'will-prayer'. At any given time we do not know what more we are capable of tomorrow, but there is no reason for us, equally, to exaggerate the facts as they are. Even more important than either our changing perspective of tomorrow's possibilities or our present view of today's actualities, is our need to see beyond ourselves altogether. We must lift ourselves from the egotism of the shadow to the egoity of that which looks towards the light and which at some point is absorbed in its selfless expansive wonderment at the one supreme, single light of spirit. If this is what we are required to do, we have got to give up any sense of identity. It is more difficult to give up a sense of identity when it is bound up with good qualities, with our spiritual assets and whatever we have worked towards for so long. All of these have got to go. One has to train oneself to be established in a state of mind with no expectations. Without expectations we are less liable to distort and obscure what is going on, because what is going on manifests on many levels. What is going on involves maya. Though this maya veils and we add to maya by projecting and fantasizing, it is also possible to use maya to reveal what is relevant and what is at the very core.

This therapeutic art involves training, and it cannot come if one is either blinded by the film of one's own goodness or the nightmare of one's own badness. One must see a whole universe of myriads of selves and monads, and the saga of humanity as a vast, essentially untold and unfinished story. At any given moment what is unmanifest is most important and what people are feeling deep down is more important than what they say. What they are unable to think in the language that they use, and which somehow negates their thoughts even if it only makes them tired and go to sleep, still comes closer to the ground of being as the field of abstract potential. Coming to see it as a living realm of awareness is to function on the truly causal plane. We may thus come closer to those beings who initiate potent and beneficent causes upon the human scene. We might even make that difference to the soul of another human being which may not show for many future lives, but which could eventually be crucial.

We do not know all the arithmetic — how it all adds up, how it interconnects — but we prevent ourselves from knowing a great deal that we could know by imposing expectations, by over-analysis, but above all by a false dramatization of our personal egos. If we can *let go* of all of these, and if we can look beyond and behind the shadow play of personal selves, we can see in the divine dark the mighty manifestation of the great hosts represented by Krishna, the Logos, the Christos. We can see this in ourselves, even if the only way we can see it in ourselves is by making it a point. Before we can make it a point, we have to reduce our composite astral form to a cipher. We have to void the very language and categories of the personal self. An ancient scripture teaches that any feeling of like or dislike reinforces, expands, aggravates that shadow. Pandit Bhavani Shankar suggests that when one enters the spiritual path and reaches the *karana sharira*, one reads therein the archetypal origins of like and dislike. They are much more difficult to understand than their materialized manifestations. Attraction towards existence and aversion from non-existence bind the individuality itself. Their personal reflection is a pseudo-attraction and a pseudo-repulsion that maximizes the elemental interaction of the shadow. This has to be cut at the root. One has to go beyond 'history' to see all events as participating in a common medium, all beginnings and endings as existing merely in the region of form. One has to gain that unbroken consciousness which does not participate in succession, in simultaneity, in contrast or comparison. One of the necessary steps to get to this stage is to see beyond the deceptive contrasts of good and evil as pictured by the personal self. One must become so humble before universal welfare that one can only say one does not know what is the supreme criterion of the sum-total of human good, of the optimal use of everything.

This perspective is radically different from our ordinary way of looking at the world, where we have elaborated our childhood fears and traumas and created notions of success and failure which have bound us. We must get away from this altogether, voiding it in our consciousness. In the beginning you have to reach, even if you cannot go beyond, that point where in the very act of reaching you render obeisance — in the words of the *Gita*, a long prostration — devoted service to those Mahatmas who embody *par excellence* the *yajna* of *Jnana Yoga*. If you do the best you can, and lose yourself in the adoration of those who do so much more, a sort of healing takes place. There is a progressive dissolution of the personal self and a gradual atrophy or dying out of *ahankara*, the 'I'-making faculty.

It will take time for this process to work itself out fully, because every now and again you will be tempted, like a miser counting his coins, to count your blessings in terms of some plausible story of your progress over a period of seven years, over a lifetime, over the remaining length of time until the moment of death, linking this up to some notion of before and after. The moment you start to dwell on such thoughts, you have short-circuited the process. You have restored egotistic concern. Therefore, you will have to make the voiding of self a whole way of living that applies to everything. Initially you can apply it to one thing, two things, more things. If you can link it up to the most elementary necessities of life like waking up, going to sleep, eating and bathing — if you can link it up to these archetypal activities whereby you are discharging debts on the lower planes of consciousness — and you can do this with an awareness of the cosmic host — then in time you can make a decisive difference. In due course you can actually create out of the very ashes of your former sense of being, from a germ and an embryonic seed, a new vesture or *rupa*, a supple astral form saturated with the sacrificial energy of steadfast devotion. Its tropism will naturally help it to turn towards the holy *Hiranyagarbha*, the golden vesture of Brahma and Shiva. Mahatmas are continually engaged in giving a forward impulse to human evolution, without any attachments to the relativities and partialities of the perceptions of beings bound upon the great wheel of change.

Wisdom-Sacrifice begins where one is, but its end is beyond one's capacity to reckon or conceive. It resembles Jacob's ladder. It is the *Ahavaniya* of the Vedas, the great sacrificial ladder. It is like fire which must arise for each as a spark at some point, but which can become a leaping flame bursting the boundaries of all our maps of manifested existence. Hence it is called the fire of knowledge, the sovereign purifier. There is something about fire that is non-discriminatory. It is involved in a relentless process of purgation. Self-conscious participation in the cosmic fire of universal sacrifice is the great privilege offered in an initiatory mode by Shiva to Bhringi, by Vasishtha to Rama, by Krishna to Arjuna, by Buddha to Subhuti, and to all those deserving disciples who could use the sacred teaching for the sake of adding to the sum of universal good.

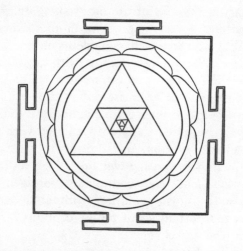

# RETURN TO SHIVA

## FROM THE YOGA VASISHTHA

# I
# ARUPA BRAHMA

Rama said: You have declared the mind to be a pure essence, unconnected with this earth or matter, and verily Brahmā itself.

Tell me, O Brahmin, why remembrance of former births is not the cause of Brahmā's birth, as it is with you and me.

Vasishtha replied: Whoever has had a body accompanied by acts in a prior existence retains its reminiscence, and this is the cause of rebirth.

But Brahmā is known to have had no prior acts and thus cannot have any reminiscence.

Existing by its own mind alone, Divine Spirit is Self-born and is its own cause.

Everlasting, with body born of itself from the Self-existent Brahman, the Self-born Brahmā has no body except the subtle *ativahika*.

Rama said: The everlasting subtle body or *sukshma sarira* and the mortal body or *sthula deha* are distinct. Do all created beings have a subtle body like that of Brahmā?

Vasishtha replied: All beings produced by a cause have *sukshma* and *sthula* bodies. But the Unborn Causeless has only one body — the *ativahika* or everlasting spiritual body.

The uncreated Brahmā, the cause of all created beings, having no cause of itself, has only one body.

The prime Lord of creatures has no material body but manifests in the aerial forms of his spiritual body.

This body, composed of mind alone, is without contact with earth or matter. From it the first Lord spreads forth the world.

All creatures are but forms of the ideas in that mind, being without other basis and coeval in essence with their cause.

That uncreated Being of perfect intelligence is purely of the form of mind, having intellectual but not material body.

This First Cause of all productions in the material world is Self-born through the prime moving force in the form of mind.

By the first impulse of that force the expanse of creation was spread out, as wind and wave move in proportion to the impetus they receive.

This shining creation, brilliant to sight, derives its light from the luminous mind of *Arupa* Brahmā, and appears real only to our conception.

As in a dream vision of enjoyment of connubial bliss, unreal objects of desire present themselves as actualities to our false and fond imagination.

The empty, immaterial and formless Spirit is represented as the Self-born manifest Lord of creatures, existing in the form of the First Male.

Undiscerned as pure intelligence, It manifests to all by the evolution of its volition. Indistinct as absolute rest, It is resplendent in the display of its nature.

Brahmā is the divine power of volition and is personified as the Protogonos devoid of material body. Purely of the form of mind, it is the sole cause of the triple worlds.

Its volition produces the exertion of the energies of the Self-born, just as human desires impel mankind to action and the vacuous mind manifests as a mountain of desires.

Forgetting its everlasting and incorporeal nature, it assumes a solid material body, showing itself as delusive appearances.

But Brahmā of unsullied understanding is not involved in self-oblivion by transformation from the *nirguna* to the *saguna* state.

Unborn of matter, Brahmā sees no apparition, unlike those exposed by their ignorance to misleading errors of falsehood looming as mirages before them.

Brahmā is purely of the form of mind, and not composed of matter. The world as the product of Eternal Mind is of the same nature as its archetype.

Just as the uncreated Brahmā is without secondary cause, so the creation is without any cause but Brahmā.

There is no difference of product and producer, for works are as perfect as their authors.

No cause and effect are to be found within this creation, because the three worlds are but prototypes of the archetype of Divine Mind.

Stretched out upon the model of Divine Mind, and unformed by any other spirit, the world is immanent in that Mind like fluidity in water.

Mind spins out the extended unreality of the world like a castle in the air or a utopian city.

There is no materiality. It is as false as the snake in the rope. Hence it is in no way possible for Brahmā or other things to exist as individual bodies.

Even spiritual bodies are non-existent to those of enlightened understanding. Material bodies are totally unreal.

Man or *manu* derives from *manas* and is a form of the volitional soul *virinchi* with dominion over the mental world — *manorajyam*.

*Manas* is Brahmā called *virinchi* by the exercise of its inherent *sankalpa sisriksha* or incipient creative volition. It displays itself as the visible world through development of its own essence.

This *virinchi*, or creative power, and *manas* are consubstantial and unconnected with matter which is a mere creation of fancy.

All visible things are contained in the bosom of mind, just as the lotus bud and blossom reside in the lotus seed. Hence the mental and visible existence of things are the same.

The objects of your dreams, the desires of your heart, the ideals of your imagination, together with your ideas, notions and impressions of visible things — know them all to be within the receptacle of mind.

But visible things bound up with mental desire are as baneful to their beholder as an apparition to a child.

The ideal origin of phenomena develops itself like the germ in the seed which becomes a great tree.

Without reliance on the Self, there can be no peace with phenomena full of troubles, nor solace for the mind. The feeling of perception of visibles will never be lost to the perceiver. Abstraction from it alone is liberation.

Utpatti Khanda, III

# II
# THE JIVANMUKTA

Rama asked: Tell me, O Teacher, what is distinctive to the experience of liberation by the living and by the disembodied, so that I may learn with an understanding lit up by the light of Holy Writ.

Vasishtha answered: Whosoever remains as he is, unperturbed, continuing intact in a state of voidness in the midst of society, such a one is a Jivanmukta.

Whosoever is engaged in his intellection alone and seems to be sleeping in his waking state, while conducting his worldly affairs, such a one is a Jivanmukta.

Whose countenance is neither flushed nor pallid in joy or grief, and who is constant in contentment with what he gets, such a one is a Jivanmukta.

Whose waking is as a state of sound sleep, and who is not awake to the accidents of the waking state, and whose waking state is insensible to the desires incident to it, such a one is a Jivanmukta.

Who though actuated by the feelings of affection, repulsion, fear and the like, remains serene, and as calm and unmoved as the void within himself, such a one is a Jivanmukta.

Who has no trace of pride in him, and has no conceit in him when he acts or when he refrains from acting, such a one is a Jivanmukta.

Who at one glance or winking of his eye, sees entire the creation and the dissolution of the world, enclosed within the Supreme Self, such a one is a Jivanmukta.

Who is feared by none and is never afraid, and who is freed from the emotions of joy, anger and fear, such a one is a Jivanmukta.

Who is quiet and quietly disposes his business in this world, who stands as an individual in the sight of men and yet is unattached to any sense of self, who though a sentient being is insensible to all impressions, such a one is a Jivanmukta.

Who being full of all possessions and having everything present before him, remains aloof and apathetic to them as if they were useless to him, such a one is a Jivanmukta.

24

Having spoken of the embodied Jivanmukta, I will now tell you about the disembodied liberation, which like a breath of wind enters into the soul when it is loosened from the mortal body.

The disembodied free spirit neither rises nor sets nor does it wane, it is neither manifest nor hidden, it is not at a distance, nor is it in me, nor there, nor in any other person.

It shines forth in the form of the sun and it preserves the world in the manner of Vishnu. It creates the world in the shape of the lotus-born Brahmā. It destroys all as Rudra-Shiva.

It takes the form of the sky supported on the shoulders of air, which upholds all living beings — the gods, sages and demi-gods in the three worlds. It takes the form of boundary mountains and separates the different regions.

It becomes the earth and supports these numerous sets of beings, it takes the form of trees, plants and grass, yielding fruits and grains for the sustenance of all.

It takes the forms of fire and water and burns and melts therein. It sheds ambrosia in the form of the moon, and causes death in the shape of poison.

It becomes light wherewith it fills the space of the firmament, and spreads darkness in the form of *tamas*. It becomes emptiness to leave space for all, while in the form of the hills it hinders free movement on earth.

In the form of the fleet mind, it propels the self-moving creatures, and in the form of dull matter it settles the inert immovables. It girds the earth by its form of the ocean, as a bracelet encircles the arm.

The bodiless Spirit takes upon itself the great body of the sun and illuminates all the worlds with their minute particles, while it remains quiet in itself.

Whatever is or ever was shining in this universe, or is to be, in present, past and future times, know them all, O Rama, as forms of the Divine Spirit.

Utpatti Khanda, IX

# THAT WHICH ABIDES

**R**ama said: That which abides during *Mahapralaya* is commonly called a formless void. Why do you say there is then no void, nor light nor darkness either?

How could that state be without the intellect and the living principle, and how could the entities of mind and understanding be wanting in it? How could there be nothing and not all things? These paradoxes in your teachings confuse me.

The Sage Vasishtha said: You have raised a difficult question, Rama, but I shall solve it as easily as the sun dispels darkness. Upon the termination of the great *Kalpa* age there abides the divine TAT SAT, which cannot be termed a void, as I shall now explain. Attend, O Rama, and listen.

This world inheres in the TAT SAT like images carved in relief upon a pillar, and cannot be said to be a void. Again, wherever there is a representation of the plenum, designated as the world, whether illusory or not, it could not be a void or emptiness.

As a pillar with carved or painted figures upon it cannot be said to be devoid of them, so Brahmā exhibiting the worlds contained in itself cannot be a void. But the worlds contained in Brahmā become both a something and a nothing, like billows in calm water which may either exist or not exist.

Again, it happens in some places that certain forms are marked upon insensible trees by the hand of time, which people then mistake for images; just so it comes to pass that certain forms of evanescent matter arise in eternal mind which people then mistake for reality. These comparisons of the carved pillar and the tree with the world are partial and incomplete, and refer only to the presence of the transient world within the permanent Brahmā.

The appearance of the world has no external cause. It rises, endures and sets spontaneously and of itself in the self-same nature of Brahmā. It is the character of the Divine Soul and Mind to raise and dispel by turns such images within themselves, just like the creations of our imagination. The connotation of the term 'void' or *sunya* as the opposite of 'existence' or *asunya* is a fiction as false as emptiness is absent in nature. Something must come from something, nor can nothing be reduced to nothing at *Mahapralaya*.

Concerning the absence of darkness, the divine light of Brahmā is not like the light of a material luminary. The everlasting light cannot be obscured by darkness as can sunshine, moonlight, the blazing of a fire or the twinkling of stars in our eyes. The absence of the light of the great celestial luminaries is called darkness, and there being no materiality in the subtle divine nature, there can be no such darkness or light within it prior to manifestation.

The light of the formless Brahmā is an internal perception of the soul, felt and perceived only within oneself and never externally by anyone; nor is this spiritual light ever obscured by any mist or darkness of temporal objects. The indestructible Brahmā is beyond and free from external visible light and darkness, and is above the region of vacuum contained in its bosom which contains the universe sheathed within its hollow womb.

As there is no difference between the inside and outside of a fruit, there is no shade of difference between Brahmā and the universe. As the wave is contained in and composed of water, and the pot is of the earth, the world being contained in Brahmā cannot be termed null and void, but is full of Divine Spirit.

But these comparisons with earth and water do not convey the spiritual divine nature, whose formless Spirit contains and comprises the whole within itself, as do these elements their component parts and products. As the sphere of Intellect is clearer and brighter by far than even the spheres of air and *Akasha*, so the sense and idea of the world as situated in Divine Mind is clearer in a far greater degree than any idea to be drawn from the visible world.

Just as it is said that the pungency of pepper is perceived by one who tastes it, and not by him who has never tasted it, so the nature of Intellect is known in the intellectual sphere only by cultivated intellect and by none who are without it. Thus the Intellect appears as no intellect to one who is devoid of intelligence, and this world is perceived within Divine Spirit or otherwise, according as one has cultivated or neglected spiritual knowledge.

Thus the world is seen either in its outward form or in a spiritual light as the same or other than Brahmā; but the Yogi views it in the *Turiya* state of cessation within his still soul. The Yogi, though leading a secular life, abides with soul fixed and mind tranquil. He lives like Brahmā, unknown to and unnoticed by others;

knowing all and filled with wisdom, he is a treasury of knowledge unknown to the rest of mankind.

As waves of various shapes rise and fall in the still and shapeless breast of the sea, innumerable worlds of various forms float within the unaltered and formless space of Brahmā's bosom. From the fullness of *Brahmatma* proceeds the fullness of *Jivatma*, which is also formless. This aspect of Brahmā is said to derive from its purpose of Self-manifestation.

The totality of worlds proceeding from the plenum of Brahmā, there remains the same sum total in that plenitude of Brahmā itself. Considering the world as synonymous with Brahmā in our minds, we discover their identity, just as by taste we find the pepper and its pungency to be the same.

Given the illusory nature of finite minds and their objects, their reflections upon each other are as empty as the shadows of shadows. Know Brahmā as smaller than the smallest atom and the most minute of particles. It is purer than air and more tranquil than the subtle aether embosomed within it.

Unbounded by space and time, its form is the most expansive of all. Without beginning or end, it is an Ineffable Light without brightness. Its form is that of Intellect and Life Eternal, without the conditions and accidents of living beings. Eternal Will abides in Divine Mind, devoid of the desires of finite minds.

Without the manifestation of Intellect there is neither vitality nor understanding, neither intellection nor any organic action and sensation, and no mental desire or feeling at all. Hence that Being, full of these powers, without decline or decay, is seen by us to be established in a state of formless tranquillity more pure than the rarefied vacuum of the aethereal regions.

Rama said: Tell me again the exact form of this transcendental Being having the nature of infinite Intelligence, to shed more light upon my understanding.

Vasishtha said: I have told you often that there is one Supreme Brahmā, the cause of causes, which abides alone in itself when the universe is finally absorbed or dissolved into it. Hear me describe it fully to you.

That which the Yogi in his *Samadhi* sees within himself, after forgetting his personality and repressing the faculties and functions of his mind, is verily the form of that unspeakable Being. As the

Yogi absorbed in *Samadhi*, abstracted from the visible world and in privation of viewer and the viewed, sees light shining in himself, even such is the form of that Being.

He who forgets the nature of *jiva* and all proclivities towards intelligible forms, yet abides in the pure light and tranquil state of his intellect, is the form of the Supreme Spirit. He who has no feeling of the breathing of the winds nor of the touch or pressure of anything upon his body, but lives as a mass of intelligence, is the form of the Supreme.

Again, that state of mind which a man of sense enjoys in long and sound sleep, undisturbed by dreams or gnats, is the form of the Supreme. That which abides in the hearts of vacuum, air, and stone and is the intelligence of all inanimate beings, is the form of the Supreme. Again, whatever irrational, insensible beings live in nature, without soul or mind, the tranquil state of their existence is the nature of the Supreme Soul.

That which is seated in the midst of the intellectual light of the soul, the aethereal light of the sun, and the light of our vision, is verily the form of the Supreme. The soul witnessing knowledge, the solar and visual lights, and darkness, is without beginning and end and is the form of the Supreme.

That which manifests the world to us, remaining hidden from view, whether the same or other than the world, is the form of the Supreme. That which though filled with activity is as unmoved as a stone, and which though not a void appears as an empty vacuum, is the form of the Supreme.

That which is the source and end of our triple consciousness of knower, known and knowledge is most difficult to attain. The form of the Supreme shines forth in the triple conditions of knowable, knower and knowledge, displaying them as a vast insensible mirror. Understand it not as the cause — *nimatta* — but as the source — *vivarta* — of the triple category.

The mind freed from bodily activities and dreams, concentrated in the intellect and present alike in all moving and unmoving things, is said to abide even beyond the end of our being. The intelligent mind fixed in immovability and freed from the exercise of its faculties is assimilated to the Divine Mind.

Utpatti Khanda, X

# IV

# CHINTAMANI

The Sage Vasishtha said: The universe rose to being from the perfect quiescence and tranquillity of the supremely holy Spirit, in the manner which you must now hear with your finest understanding and attention.

As sound sleep displays itself in visionary dreams, so does Brahmā manifest himself in the works of creation, of which he is the soul and receptacle.

The world is outwardly ever evolving in its course, but inherently it is identical with that Being whose form is one with the ineffable glory of *Chintamani* — the eternal Jewel of Intellect.

*Chit*, or Intellect, produces a reflection of itself within itself, prior to its manifestation as either consciousness or knowledge of egoism.

This reflective intellect then apprehends subtle natures purer and finer than aether, but which receive their names and forms only later.

Next, the transcendental principle becomes rational intellect, eager for thought. It is appropriately termed *Chit* on account of its exhibition of what is called intelligence.

Lastly, it takes the form of concrete consciousness and receives the name *jiva*, or living soul. Reflecting upon itself, it veils its divine nature.

This living principle becomes involved in thoughts relating only to the world, yet it depends in its nature upon Divine Being.

Then there arises into being *kham*, the aether, which is the seed or source of the property of sound, and which afterwards becomes the bearer of meanings.

Next, the elements of egoism and duration are produced within the *jiva*. These two are the roots of the subsistence of future worlds.

This ideal knowledge of the illusive forms of the network of the world within Divine Spirit is made to appear as a reality by the omnipotent power.

Thus Ideal Self-Consciousness becomes the seed of the tree of desires swayed by the egoism subsisting in the aether.

Intellect in the form of the aethereal ego dwells on the element of sound — *shabda tanmatra*. Becoming by degrees more dense than the rarefied aether, it produces the element of mind.

Sound is the seed of words, which become diversified as names, nouns and significant terms. The assemblage of words, resembling the foliage of a tree, is varied through inflections, sentences and collections into *Vedas* and *Shastras*.

All these worlds derive their beauty from the Supreme Spirit, and thus the multitude of words, full of meanings, become widely spread at last.

Intellect having this family as its offspring is designated by the term *jiva*, which then becomes the tree of all types of beings known under a variety of expressions bearing significations.

Afterwards, the fourteen kinds of living beings, filling every position of every world, spring from this *jiva*.

Then Intellect, by a motion and inflation of itself, and at an instantaneous thought, becomes the air, the *tanmatra* of touch and feeling, but which is still without its name and activity.

The air, which is the seed of the tree of tangibles, then develops itself into branches composed of the forty-nine kinds of wind, the causes of the breathings and motions of all beings.

Intellect next produces, at its own pleasure and from its own idea of light, the *tanmatra* of lustre, which later receives its diverse designations.

Then the sun, fire, lightning and other seeds of the tree of light cause the various colours of the bodies that fill the world.

Reflecting upon the absence of fluidity, Intellect then produces the liquid body of waters, whose taste constitutes the *tanmatra* of flavour.

The desire of the soul for different flavours is the seed of the tree of taste, and it is by the relish of a variety of tastes that the world is made to go on in its course.

Then the self-willed Brahmā, wishing to produce the visible earth, causes the property of smell to pertain to it through his own *tanmatra* of solidity.

Having made his elementary solidity the seed of the tree of forms, he makes his *tanmatra* of roundness the substratum of the spherical world.

All these *tanmatras* being evolved from Intellect are of themselves eventually involved back into Intellect, like bubbles arising and subsiding in water.

In this manner, they abide in combined states until their final resolution into their simple and separate natures.

They are all mere forms and formations of pure Intellect, remaining within the sphere of divine intelligence just as the germs of the great banyan tree reside in the pollen and seed.

Sprouting forth in time, they burst into a hundred branches; having been concealed in an atom, they become as large as if to last forever.

Such is the growth and multiplication of things through the pervasion of Intellect, until they are arrested by its contraction. Then, weakened by its withdrawal, they all languish.

Thus the *tanmatras* are produced in Intellect out of its own volition, and manifest as formless scintillas.

These fivefold elements are verily the only seeds of all things in the world, bearing the impetus given them in the beginning. To our apprehension, they are the seeds of elementary bodies, but in their true natures they are uncreated ideal facets of Intellect replenishing the world.

Utpatti Khanda, XII

# V

# THE MIND OF SHIVA

The Sage Vasishtha said: Know, Sinless Rama, that whosoever thinks of any thing, in any manner at any place or time, he comes to experience the same in the same manner in the same place and time.

Destructive poison becomes ambrosia to venomous insects who take it to be their dainty nourishment. An enemy becomes your friend by your friendly behaviour towards him.

In whatever manner all beings consider themselves and others for any length of time, they seem to be so, by their mode and habit of thinking, as if this were by an act of destiny.

The manner in which the active Intellect — *Chit* — represents a thing in the soul, the same is imprinted in the consciousness — *samvid* — of its own nature.

When our consciousness represents the twinkling of an eye as a *Kalpa*, we are led to believe a single moment to be an age of long duration.

When we are conscious of a *Kalpa* as a twinkling, the *Kalpa* age is thought to pass as a moment, just as a long night in our unconscious sleep appears as but a moment upon awakening.

The night appears an endless age to the long-suffering sick, while it seems but a moment in the nightly revels of the merry. A moment appears as an age in a dream, while an age passes away as a moment in the state of sleep.

The notions of the resurrection of the dead, of metempsychosis, of being reborn in a new body, of being a boy, youth or old man, and of journeying hundreds of leagues to different places, all are but phenomena of sleep and retrospective visions in a dream.

King Harischandra is said to have thought a single night to be a dozen years, and Ravana seemed to pass his long life of a hundred years in a single night.

What was a moment to Brahmā was the whole age and lifetime of Man; and what is a day to Vishnu constitutes the long life of Brahmā.

The whole lifetime of Vishnu is but one day to the seated Shiva, for one whose mind is motionless in fixed meditation is not conscious of changes of days, nights, seasons and years.

There is no substance nor substantial world in the mind of the meditative Yogin to whom the sweet pleasures of the world appear as bitter and the bane of true felicity.

The bitter seems sweet by thinking it so; what is unfavourable comes to be favourable, as that which is friendly becomes unfriendly by being taken in its contrary sense.

Therefore, O Rama, it is by persistent meditation that we acquire the abstract knowledge of things, just as what we have learned we forget through lack of recapitulation.

It is by regulated thought that we may find all things to be in a state of positive rest. The unthinking fall into the errors of the revolving world, like a boat passenger who thinks the land and the objects on the shore are receding or revolving around him.

Thus the unquestioning portion of mankind, wandering in error, think the world is moving around them, but the discerning mind sees the whole as an empty void filled with phantoms as in a dream.

It is erroneous thought that shows the white as black or blue. It is mistaken judgment that leads one to rejoice or grieve at the events of life.

The unthinking are led to imagine a house where there is none; the ignorant are infatuated by belief in phantoms, and are the slayers of their own lives.

It is reminiscence, or memory, who projects the dream as her consort, and represents things as presented to it by thoughts of the waking state.

The dream is as unreal as the empty vacuum, abiding in the hollow sphere of the intellectual soul. It overspreads the mind like the shadow of a cloud, filling it with images like those of a puppet under a magic lantern.

Know the phenomena of the revolving worlds to be no more than the effects of the vibrations of the mind in the empty space of the soul, similar to the motions and gestures of hobgoblins fancied by a child.

As this is but a magical illusion, without substance or basis in itself, all these imposing scenes of vision are merely the empty and aerial sights of dreams.

Just as the waking man beholds the wondrous world before him,

34

so also does the sleeping man perceive the same. Both resemble the insensible pillar which has the images of statues engraved upon it.

The mighty pillar of the Divine Spirit has carved upon itself the future of the created world, just as I may see a troop of men passing before me in a dream.

Thus the waking world sleeps in the soul of Brahmā, and springs from his mind, as the vegetable world rises from the sap hidden in the earth which gives life and vernal splendour.

Thus the whole world is concealed and arises within the Supreme Spirit, as the brightness of golden ornaments is contained in and comes out of the auric metal.

Every atom of creation resides in the plenum of Divine Spirit, just as all the members of the body repose in the person of their possessor.

The visible world bears the same relation to the bodiless and undivided Divine Spirit as the man struggling in a dream has to his antagonist.

Thus the real and the unreal, the spirit and the world, and all things sink into the void at the great *Kalapanta* destruction of the universe, save and except the Divine Intellect which encloses the world in itself.

It cannot both be true that the One is the cause and that the world is unreal. There is no other cause than Brahman, the ALL.

Utpatti Khanda LX

# VI

# TRANSMUTATION OF MIND

The Sage Vasishtha said: Attend, O Raghava, to this question I asked of Lotus-born Brahmā. I spoke, saying: O Lord, you declare the irrevocable power of curses and incantations; yet it is said men may frustrate their force.

We have witnessed the power of spells, pronounced by potent *mantras*, to overwhelm the understanding and senses of living creatures.

We see in this as intimate a union of mind with body, as motion with air, or fluidity with the sesamum seed.

There are, it seems, no bodies apart from the creations of mind, like fancied chimeras in visions and dreams, false sights of water in mirages, or an appearance of two moons in the sky.

Why else does dissolution of the one bring on extinction of the other, just as quietude of mind is followed by loss of bodily sensation?

Tell me, O Lord, whether mind may remain unmoved by the power of sense-subduing incantations and curses, or whether mind and sense being one, they are overpowered together.

Lord Brahmā replied: Know that nothing in the treasure-house of this world is unattainable by man through rightful exertion.

Know also that all species of beings, from the state of highest Brahmā down to minute insects, are endowed with the aspects of mind and body.

The mind is ever active and changing, while the worthless body of flesh is dull and inert.

The fleshy body accompanying all living creatures is overpowered by the influence of curses and spells, practised by the art of incantation — *abhichara vidya*.

The influence of certain subtle powers can stupefy a man, making him dull and dumb. Spell-bound persons deprived of their external senses may droop insensible, and fall down like drops of water from a lotus leaf.

But the mind is ever free and unsubdued, though subject to the influence of all living beings in the three worlds.

He who controls his mind by perpetual patience and incessant vigilance is a man of impregnable character, unapproachable by calamity.

The more a man engages in the proper employment of his mind, the more he is successful in obtaining the end he holds in view.

Mere physical force is never successful in any undertaking; mental activity alone assures success in all attempts.

When the attention of the mind is directed to incorporeal ends, it is as vain to attempt to harm it as to pierce a stone with an arrow.

Drown the body in water, bury it in mud, burn it in fire or fling it aloft in the air, yet the mind is not turned from its pole. He who is true to his purpose is sure of success.

Intense bodily effort may overcome impediments, but mental exertion alone leads to ultimate success in every undertaking.

Recall the instance of the storied Indra, who directed every thought to the assimilation of himself into the very image of his beloved, drowning all his bodily pains in the bliss of her remembrance.

Think on the manly fortitude of Mandavya, who made his mind as callous as marble, and was insensible to suffering when beheaded.

Think of the sage who fell into a dark pit while his whole mind remained intent on his sacred rites, and entered heaven by the merit of his mental sacrifice.

Remember how the sons of Indu attained to my state by the power of persevering devotion, which even I cannot avert.

Hosts of sages and adepts, gods and men, by never laying aside their mental energies, have been crowned with success in their pursuits.

No pain or sickness, no incantation or curse, no malicious beast or evil spirit can break down the resolute mind, any more than a blow with a lotus leaf can split the breast of a boulder.

Those you have seen shaken by trials and persecutions, I understand as too infirm in their faith, and weak in their minds and manliness.

Men of mental vigilance are never trapped by the snare of error in this perilous world; they are not visited by the demon of despair in their waking or sleeping state.

Therefore, let a man employ himself in the exercise of his own manly powers, employing his mind and mental energy in noble pursuits, in paths of truth and holiness.

The enlightened mind sheds its former darkness, seeing its objects in their true light; thoughts that grow great in the mind absorb it at last, just as the fancy of a ghost lays hold of the mind of a child.

New reflections efface prior impressions from the tablet of mind, as an earthen pot turning on the potter's wheel no more thinks itself mere clay.

The mind, O *Muni*, is transmuted instantly into its pellucid form, as the light and airy fountain spray suddenly glistens with the sun's brightness.

Averse to right inquiry, the purblind mind sees all in darkness, even in the midst of day, and at night is deceived by the delusion of twin moons.

Whatever the mind holds in view, it soon succeeds in accomplishing, and, as it does aught of good or evil, it reaps rewards of gladness or bitterness in the soul.

A faulty mirror reflects a thing in a false light, as a distracted lover sees flames in moonbeams, which burn and consume him in his state of distraction.

It is mental conception that makes salt seem sweet, from its giving a flavour to salted food for our joy and delight.

It is our mental conception that makes us see forests in the fog or towers in the clouds, seeming to rise and fall by turns.

In this manner, whatever shape the imagination gives to a thing, it appears in the same visionary guise before the sight of the mind. Therefore, knowing this world of your imagination to be neither reality nor unreality, forebear to accept it, with its various shapes and colours, merely as it appears to view.

Utpatti Khanda, XCII

# VII
# JNANA AND AJNANA

Rama said: Tell me, O Sage, the grounds of *Yoga* meditation, which produce the seven kinds of consummation aimed at by adepts in *Yoga*. Being best acquainted with all recondite truths, you must know this better than all other men.

Vasishtha replied: These grounds consist of seven states of ignorance — *ajnana bhumi* — and as many of knowledge — *jnana bhumi*. These again diverge into many others by their mutual intermixture.

All these states, deep-rooted in the nature of man — *maha satta* — either by habit — *pravritti* — or by training — *sadhana*, produce their respective fruits in time.

Attend now to the seven-fold grounds of *ajnana*, and you will come to know thereby the nature of the seven-fold grounds of *jnana*.

Know these definitions of *jnana* and *ajnana* to be the briefest lesson I will give you: abiding in one's own true nature — *swarupa*, constitutes the highest *jnana* and emancipation; divergence from this into egoism — *ahanta* — is the root of *ajnana*, error, and bondage in this world.

Those who do not deviate from consciousness of their true nature — *samvritti swarupa* — as composed of essentially pure being — *suddha sanmatra* — are not liable to *ajnana*, all passions and affections, feelings of envy and enmity, being extinct in them.

Falling off from *samvritti swarupa*, and diving into the intellect or *Chit*, pursuing conceptions of cognizable objects, is the greatest *ajnana* and error of mankind.

Know the equipoise of the mind between past thoughts of some object and future thoughts of another object, the respite of the mind's thinking, to be the repose of the soul in *samvritti swarupa*.

That calm state of the soul following the cessation of thoughts and desires in the mind, cold and quiet as the bosom of a stone yet without the torpor of sleep or dull drowsiness, is called the resting of the soul in the recognition of itself.

When devoid of all sense of egoism and emptied of all cognizance of duality, when indistinct from the Universal Soul and shining forth with the light of unsleeping intelligence, then the soul is said to rest in *swarupa*.

But this state of the pure self-intelligent soul is obscured by the various states of *ajnana*, which I will now relate to you. These include the three states of wakefulness known as embryonic waking — *vijajagrat*, ordinary waking — *jagrat*, and intense waking — *mahajagrat*.

Also included are the three states of dreaming — *swapna*, waking dream and sleepy waking, as well as sound sleep — *sushupti*. These then are the seven grounds of *ajnana*.

These seven, productive of sheer *ajnana*, when joined with one another become manifold through mixture, and are known by many names.

In the beginning was intelligent Intellect — *Chaitanya Chit*, which gave rise to nameless and pure Intellect — *Suddha Chit*, which became the source of mind and living soul.

This Intellect remains as the ever-waking embryonic seed of all, wherefore it is called the waking seed — *vijajagrat*. Since it is the first condition of cognition, it is termed the primal waking state.

Know that the ordinary waking state — *jagrat* — is next to the primal divine waking intelligence. It consists of belief in the individual personality, and the thought, "I am this, and these things are mine by chance."

The glaring or great waking state — *mahajagrat* — consists in the firm belief, "I am this, and these things are mine by virtue of Karmic merit in this or previous lives."

Cognition of anything as real, either by bias — *rudhadhyasa*, or by mistake — *arudha*, is called waking dream. This includes such states as the appearance of twin moons in the sky, of silver in shells, of water in mirages, and also the imaginary castles built by daydreamers.

Sleeping dreams are of many kinds, as is known upon awakening. Their truth is doubtful owing to the shortness of their duration.

Reliance placed upon things seen in dreams, after awakening from sleep, is called waking dream, and persists only through its remembrance in the mind.

A thing long unseen and appearing dimly, like a stalwart figure in a dream, if taken for an actual entity of the waking state, is also called a waking dream.

Dreams dreamt either in the living body or in the dead body of the dreamer appear as phantoms of the waking state.

Besides these six states there is also a torpid or *jada* state of the living soul, called *sushupti*, or sound sleep, in which the soul can sense its future pleasures and pains.

In this last state of the soul all outward objects, from a straw up to a mountain, appear to be mere atoms of dust, just as the mind views the world as minute during profound meditation.

O Rama, I have told you in brief the chief features of *jnana* and *ajnana*, but each of these states branches out into a hundred forms with various traits of their own.

A long continued waking dream is accounted as the waking state — *jagrat*, and becomes differentiated through the diversity of its objects.

*Jagrat* contains the conditions of the divine wakeful soul, but also many conditions which mislead men from one error to another, as a storm casts boats into whirlpools and eddies.

Some lengthened dreams in sleep seem like the waking sights of daylight; while others, though seen in the broad daylight of the waking state, are no better than night dreams seen by day, and are termed daydreams.

Thus have I related to you the seven grounds of *ajnana*, along with all their varieties. They are to be carefully avoided by the right use of reason and by the sight of the Supreme Soul within.

Utpatti Khanda, CXVII

# VIII

# THE SEVEN STAGES OF COGNITION

The Sage Vasishtha said: O Sinless Rama, attend now to the sevenfold stages of cognition, knowing which, you will no more plunge into the mire of ignorance. Disputants are apt to speak of many more stages of *Yoga* meditation, but I hold these seven to be sufficient for the attainment of the chief good or ultimate emancipation.

Knowledge is understanding and consists of acquaintance with these seven stages only, but emancipation from transmigration is the object of knowledge and transcends such acquaintance, while knowledge of truth is ultimate emancipation itself. These three terms are synonymous, since the living being who knows the truth is freed from transmigration and thereby attains ultimate emancipation.

The grounds of knowledge are comprised first of the desire of becoming good; then comes discretion, followed by purity of mind, the third stage in the acquisition of knowledge.

The fourth is self-reliance as the true refuge; worldly indifference is the fifth. Sixth is the power of abstraction; and the final stage of knowledge is universalization of all in the One.

Emancipation lies at the end of these and is attained without difficulty after them. Attend now to the definitions of these steps, as I shall explain them unto you.

First is the desire of goodness — *subhechha* — springing from disinterest in mundane affairs, and consisting in the thought, "Why do I sit idle? I must come to know the *Shastras* in the company of good men."

The second is discretion — *vicharana* — which arises from association with wise and good men, study of the *Shastras*, and habitual aversion to worldliness; it consists in an inclination to good conduct and the doing of all sorts of good acts.

The third — *tanumanasa* — is subduing the mind and restraining it from sensual enjoyments; it is produced by the former qualities of desire for goodness and discretion.

The fourth is self-reliance, and dependence upon the Divine Spirit as the true refuge of the soul — *sattapatti*; it is attained by means of the three previous qualities.

The fifth is worldly indifference — *asansakti* — and is shown by detachment from all earthly concerns and the society of men; it arises from the previous quadruple internal delight.

By practise of these fivefold virtues, and by their attendant feelings of satisfaction and inward delight, a man is freed from his thoughts and cares of all internal and external objects.

Then comes the power of penetration into the abstract meanings of things — *padarthabhava* — the sixth step in the attainment of true knowledge, fostered by one's own exertions and the guidance of others in search of truth.

Continual practice of these six qualifications, indifference to divergences of religions, and reduction of them all to knowledge of the one true deity of nature, is universalization — *Turiyagati.*

It pertains to the nature of the living liberation of the man who beholds all things in one and the same light. Above this is the state of that glorious light itself, which is attained by the disembodied soul.

Those fortunate men, O Rama, who have arrived at the seventh stage of knowledge, are great minds who delight in the light of their souls, and have reached to their highest state of humanity.

The living liberated ones are not plunged in the waters of pleasure and sorrow, but remain calm and unmoved in both states; they are at liberty to perform or disdain the duties of their conditions and positions in society.

These men, being roused from their deep meditation by intruders, betake themselves to their secular duties like men awakening from slumber.

Being suffused by the inward delight of their souls, they feel no pleasure in the delights of the world, just as men immersed in sound sleep can feel no delight at the dalliance of beauties about them.

These seven stages of knowledge are known only to wise and thoughtful men, not to beasts, brutes and immobile entities. They are unknown to barbarians and others with barbarous minds and dispositions.

But any being who has attained to these stages of knowledge, whether beast or barbarian, embodied being or disembodied spirit, has undoubtedly obtained emancipation.

Knowledge severs the bonds of ignorance, and by loosening them produces the emancipation of our souls. It is the sole cause of removing the fallacy of the appearance of water in the mirage and similar errors.

Those who, being freed from ignorance, have not yet arrived at the ultimate perfection of disembodied liberation, have still secured the salvation of their souls by entering these stages of knowledge in their embodied state during their lifetime.

Some have passed all these stages, others two or three; some have passed the six grades, while a few have attained to the seventh state all at once.

Some have gone over three stages, others have attained the last; some have passed four stages, and some no more than one or two.

There are some who have advanced only a quarter, or half, or three-fourths of a stage. Some have passed over four quarters and a half, and some six and a half.

Common people of this earth know nothing of these travellers in the paths of knowledge, but remain blind, as though their eyes were dazzled by some planetary light, or eclipsed by its shadow.

Those wise men are compared to conquering kings, who stand victorious on these seven grounds of knowledge. The celestial elephants are as nothing beside them, and mighty warriors must bend their heads before them.

Those great minds that are victors on these grounds of knowledge are worthy of utmost veneration, as they are the conquerors of the enemies of their hearts and senses. Their rightful station is high above that of mere emperors and rulers, both in this world and in the next, both in their embodied and disembodied liberation.

Utpatti Khanda, CXVIII

# IX
# THE ATMAJNYANI

The Sage Vasishtha said: The actions the wise are seen to do — whether of goodness or otherwise, full of pleasure or pain, through whatever sort of engagement — all are as nothing and do not affect them as they would worldly mortals.

What is called action is but the exertion of mental and volitional energies, with a fixed determination and desire of performing some physical acts, which are then called the actions of a person.

The production of an act by the application of the proper means, the exertion and action of the body in conformity with one's ability, and the completion of the effect compatible with one's intention coupled with the enjoyment of the result of such agency — all these taken together are defined as action.

Regardless of whether a man is the agent in some action or not, and whether he goes to some heaven or hell, still his mind is subject to conditions precisely in accord with the desires in his heart.

The agency of the ignorant arises from their desire to do a thing, whether they accomplish it or not. It is not so with the wise, who having no such wilfulness, are not culpable for even involuntary acts. Untutored minds are full of the weeds of vice, but well cultivated souls are quite devoid of them.

The *Tattvajnyani* becomes devoid of earthly desires. Though he acts his part well, he does not long eagerly for its result. His body active, his mind remains quiet and unconcerned. All success he attributes to the will of the Divine, unlike the worldly-minded who arrogate the results to themselves though they have not the power to bring them about.

Whatever the mind intends verily comes to pass, and nothing is achieved without the application of the mind. Therefore agency belongs to the mind and not to the body.

The world proceeds from Divine Mind, is that Mind and is seated in it. Knowing all things as manifestations of the powers of that Intellect, the wise man abides in the quiescence of his desires.

The mind of the *Atmajnyani* attains perfect insensibility of desires as when a mirage of water is dissipated by rain or the morning dews are dried up by intense sun. Then the soul rests in *Turiya*.

This is neither the felicity of pleasure nor the anguish of sorrow; it consists neither in the liveliness of living beings nor in the torpidity of stones. Nor is it a mean between these antitheses, but it is in the knowing mind become *bhumananda* — the rapture of the whole earth.

The ignorant mind is transported by its thirst after the moving waters of worldly pleasures, as the elephant is misled into a foul pool where he is plunged in mud and mire but finds no real good.

Sruti declares: "A man, dreaming himself to be falling into a pit, feels the fear of his fall in his imagination, even though he is sleeping in his bed. Another man, who actually falls into a pit while fast asleep, is quite insensible of his fall." The mind paints its own pleasures and pains, not bodily action or inactivity.

Whether a man is the doer of an action or not, he perceives nothing of it when his mind is engrossed in some other thought or action. But a man views all things within himself who beholds them in the abstract meditation of his mind. The thinking mind sees outward objects as reflections of pure intellect cast without.

The *Atmajnyani*, the man knowing the knowable soul, knows himself as inaccessible to feelings of pleasure and pain. Confirmed in this knowledge, he finds no existence in anything apart from that which is contained in the container of his soul, which is like the thousandth part of a hair. This being ascertained, he views everything within himself. Certain of this knowledge, he comes to know his self as the reflector of all things and as present in them. Then comes the realization that he is not subject to pleasure or pain. Freed from all anxieties, the mind exercises its powers over all its customary duties, remaining unconcerned.

The *Atmajnyani* remains joyous even in calamity, and shines like the moon enlightening the world. He knows that his mind and not himself is the agent of his actions, though he is their doer. Knowing the agency of mind in all actions, he does not claim the merit of the exercise of his limbs, hands and feet, nor does he expect to reap all the rewards of his assiduous labours and acts.

Mental actions finding expression tend to involve their unguarded agents of ungoverned mind in the endurance of consequences. Mind is the seed of all efforts and exertions, of all acts and actions, of all results and productions. It is the source of suffering the consequences of actions. By stilling the mind, make a clean sweep of all actions. All miseries resulting from acts end with the cessation of mind. It is a practice in *Yoga* to allay the excitement of the mind with its ever-varying purposes.

A boy is led by his mind to fashion a toy, which he then dresses and paints in his play, and without showing concern or feelings of pleasure or pain, makes and breaks it as is his will. So does man build his aerial castles, and levels them without sense of gain or loss. By acting in this way in all worldly matters, no man would be spiritually entangled in them.

What cause can there be for sorrow, amidst the dangers and delights of this world, except that you have the one and not the other? What is there that is delectable or delightful or to be desired in this world that is not evanescent and perishable, except yourself? The self is neither the active nor the passive agent of your actions and enjoyments, even though actions and their fruits are attributed to it by error.

The seeming significance of actions and passions to the living soul is an illusion. Right reason shows them to have no relation to the soul. Attachment or aversion to the senses and to sensible actions and enjoyments is felt only by the sensualist, and not by those that are indifferent to sensuous affections.

There is no liberation in this world for the worldly-minded, but it is fully felt by the Yogi whose mind is freed from its attachments to the world and who abides in *Jivanmukta* — living liberation.

Though the Sage is rapt in the light of his Self-Consciousness, yet he does not fail to distinguish between unity and duality, between true entity and non-entities, or omit to view the omnipotence displayed in all the powers and potencies of nature.

To him there are no chains, no freedom, neither liberation nor bondage. The miseries of ignorance are all lost in the light of his enlightenment.

It is vain to wish for liberation when the mind is tied down to the earth. It is redundant to talk of bondage when the mind is already fastened to it. Shun both by ignoring your egoism, and remain fixed in the true Self, and continue thus to conduct yourself upon this earth with an unruffled mind.

Sthiti Khanda, XXXVIII

# X
# CHIT

The Sage Vasishtha said: Mighty Bali closed his eyes and pondered upon lotus-eyed Sukra abiding in his celestial sphere. Sukra, seated in intense meditation on the all-pervading Divine Spirit, came to know that his disciple Bali was thinking of him.

Then Sukra, the son of Brighu, whose soul is united with the boundless, omnipresent and omniscient Spirit, descended in his heavenly vesture to Bali's bright window. Bali knew his *Guru*'s form by its lustre, as the lotus knows the rising sun by its dawning rays.

He honoured his *Guru*, prostrating at his feet and placing a garland of *mandara* flowers on him as he stood before a jewelled seat. Sukra then rested on the glittering chair, bedecked with gems and *mandara* flowers, and Bali spoke to him:

Venerable Sage, the grace of your luminous presence emboldens me to address you, as the morning sunlight beckons all men to their daily work. I have become averse, O Master, to worldly enjoyments which merely delude the soul. I wish to know the truth to dispel my ignorance of myself. Tell me what these enjoyments are good for and how far they extend; and what am I, or you, or all these beings in reality?

Sukra replied: I cannot speak at length, as I must soon repair to my celestial station. Hear then, O Lord of the Daityas, what I shall state in brief. There is naught in reality but *Chit* — the Universal Intellect. All existence is this Intellect, and filled with it. So too the mind, and I, and you, and all these beings are that Intellect.

If wise, you will know you derive everything from *Chit*; otherwise, all gifts of fortune will be as useless as butter poured on ashes. It is the snare of the mind to take *Chit* as an object of thought, but the thought of its incomprehensibility liberates the soul. That inconceivable intelligence is verily the Universal Soul and the sum of all doctrines.

Know this with certainty, viewing all things in this way, and beholding the One Spirit in your spirit you will attain the state of that Infinite Spirit. Now I must return to the sky where the seven

*Munis* are assembled, and continue in the performance of my divine service.

O King, you must never abandon your duties while you are still embodied, but through your mind you may attain freedom.

So saying, Sukra rose up like a bee coated with golden lotus pollen, passing through fleecy clouds to the aureate vault of heaven, where the revolving orbs waited to receive him. After Sukra, the son of Brighu and the elder of the assembly of the gods and demigods, had departed, Bali, the best of thinking beings, reflected thus:

Truly has the *Rishi* said that *Chit* composes the three worlds, that I am *Chit*, and that it fills the four quarters showing itself in all our actions. It pervades all things within and without, and nothing is devoid of it.

Intellect perceives the sunbeams and moonbeams, for without intellectual percipience there would be no distinction between light and dark. Without perception of the earth as land there would be no distinction of earth and water nor could the term 'earth' apply to land.

If Intellect did not comprehend vast space as the quarters of the sky or mountains as great elevations of the earth, what would know those directions and mountains? If the world were not known as the world, or the void as the void, these distinctions would have no meaning.

If this large body of mine were not perceived by Intellect, how could the vestures of embodied beings be named? *Chit* resides in every organ of sense, in the body, in the mind, and in all desires. It is in both the internal and external vestures and in both being and non-being.

The Intellect forms my whole self by feeling and knowing all I feel or know; I could neither perceive nor conceive nor act through my body without the guidance of Intellect. Of what avail is this inert body, insensible as a block of wood or stone? It is *Chit*, the intelligent Spirit and Universal Soul, that makes me what I am.

I am the Intellect residing in the sun and sky and dwelling in the bodies of all beings. I am the Intellect which guides the gods and demigods, and is established alike in mobile and unmoving things. *Chit* being the sole existence, it is vain to suppose any other; and there being nought besides, there is no difference of friend and foe to us.

What if I, Bali, strike off a man's head? I cannot injure the soul present everywhere throughout space. Love and hate are properties of the soul and are not separated from it by its separation from the body. Hence the feelings and passions are inseparable from the soul.

There is nothing to be thought of except *Chit* and nothing to be obtained except the spacious womb of *Chit* comprehending the three worlds. But the passions and feelings, the mind and its powers, are mere attributes, not properties, of *Chit*, which is a wholly pure and simple essence devoid of attributes.

*Chit* is the Ego, the omnipresent, all-pervasive and ever-blissful Soul; it is beyond all other designations and without duality or division. The term *Chit* applied to the nameless power of intellection — *Chithi* — is but a verbal symbol of the omniscient and omnipresent Intelligence.

The Ego is the Supreme Lord, ever-wakeful and all-seeing, but never manifest. Purely transparent, it is beyond all appearances. All its attributes are lame, partial and imperfect. Even time, having phases and parts, is not its proper attribute. Only a mere glimmer of its light rises before us. The Eternal and Infinite Light is beyond our comprehension.

I must conceive that Ego only as the light within, distinct from all other objects of thought and without shading or colour. I salute it as *Chit* itself, and as the power of *Chithi* unaccompanied by any of its objects, established in its proper sphere.

I salute its light in me, which reveals all things to me and is beyond all thought, extending everywhere and filling space as *Chit*. It is the calm consciousness of all beings, the real Intellect, the Ego, the Mahat, infinite as space, smaller than an atom, and spreading through all alike.

I am not subject to pleasure and pain; I am conscious of no other existence than myself. I am Intelligence without any object. No worldly entity or its lack can affect me, for all possession is alien to my nature.

Knowing all things as coming from one source, there is nothing distinct from me. There is no gain or loss since the Ego always abides in all and is their all-pervading creator.

Whether I am related to various objects of thought or not matters little to me, for *Chit* is ever one though its objects are endless. As long as I am not united with the Divine Spirit, so long am I in sorrow. Speaking thus, wise Bali fell into deep meditation.

He reflected on the half-metre of Om, an emblem of the Infinite Deity, and sat quietly with all his desires and fantasies at rest. Undaunted, restraining his thoughts and thinking powers within, he remained with desires subdued, losing any distinct cognition of his meditation, of his being the meditator, and of the object of meditation.

While Bali was thus entranced beside his window decked with gems, his mind became luminous, like a lighted lamp burning with a flame unshaken by the wind. He long remained in his steady posture, like a statue carved of stone.

He sat with his mind as clear as the autumn sky, having cast off all his desires and mental anxieties, his being flooded from within by the light of spirit.

Upasama Khanda XXVI-XXVII

# XI
# ARUPA MANAS

The Sage Vasishtha said: When the Sage Vitahavya had subdued his heart and mind by the power of reason, there arose in him the qualities of universal benevolence and philanthropy.

Rama asked: Why do you say, O Sage, that the quality of benevolence sprang up in the mind of the Sage, after it had been wholly absorbed in itself through the power of reason?

Tell me, O Wise One, who is the best of speakers, how can the feelings of universal love and friendliness arise in the heart which is wholly cold and quiet, or in the mind which is entranced in the Divine Spirit?

Vasishtha replied: There are two kinds of mental extinction; one is the mind's quiescence in the living body; and the other, its absorption after the material body is dead and gone.

The possession of personal mind is the cause of woe, and its extinction is the spring of happiness; therefore one should persevere in eroding the core of this mind in order to arrive at its utter extinction.

The mind that is caught in the net of the vain desires of the world is subject to repeated births, which are the source of endless woes.

He is reckoned as a miserable being who thinks much of his person, and esteems his body as the product of the good deserts of his past lives, and who accounts his foolish and blinded personal mind as a great gift.

How can we expect the decrease of our distress as long as the mind is the concubine of the body? It is upon the letting go of this mind that the world appears to disappear before us.

Know the mind to be the root of all the miseries of life, and its desires as the sprouts of the forest of our calamities.

Rama asked: Who is it whose mind is extinct, and what is the manner of this extinction; how is its extinction brought on, and what is the nature of its annihilation?

Vasishtha replied: O sustainer of Raghu's race! I have already spoken of the nature of the mind; and you, O best of inquirers, will now hear of the means of extinguishing its impulses.

Know that mind to be paralysed and dead, which is unmoved from its steadiness by pleasure and pain, and remains as unshaken as a rock at the gentle breath of our breathing.

Know also that mind to be as dull as dead, which is devoid of any sense of separateness from others, and which is not degraded from the loftiness of its universality to the meanness of personality.

Know that mind to be dead and cold, which is not moved by difficulties and dangers, nor excited by pride and giddiness, nor elated by festivity, nor depressed by poverty and penury, and, in fine, which does not lose its serene temperament at any reverse of fortune.

Know, gentle Rama, this is what is meant by the death of the mind and the numbness of the heart; and this is the inseparable property of living liberation.

Know mindfulness of the personality to be foolishness, and unmindfulness of the same to be true wisdom. It is upon the extinction of separative mental affections that the pure essence of the mind comes to light.

This display of the intrinsic quality of the mind after the extinction of its emotions, and this temperament of the mind of the living liberated person, is regarded as the true nature of the mind.

The mind that is suffused with benevolent qualities has compassion for all living beings in nature; it is freed from the pains of repeated births in this world of woe, and is called the living liberated mind — *Jivanmukta manas.*

The nature of the living liberated mind is said to be the intrinsic essence of mind, which is replete with its holy wishes, and exempted from the doom of transmigration.

The *swarupa manas* or embodied mind is what has the notion of personality as distinct from the body; and this is essentially of the same nature as the mind of those that are liberated in their lifetime.

But when the living liberated person extinguishes all separateness in his mind, becoming within himself as joyous as moonbeams by virtue of his universal benevolence, his mind then becomes so expanded and extended that it appears to be present everywhere at all times.

The living liberated person, being unmindful of himself, becomes as cold-hearted as a plant growing in a frigid climate, with mild virtues like wintry blossoms.

The *Arupa Manas*, or Impersonal Mind, of which I have told you before, is the coolness of the disembodied soul that is altogether liberated from the consciousness of personality.

All the excellent personal virtues and qualities which reside in the embodied soul are utterly lost and absorbed into the disembodied soul, upon its liberation from the consciousness of personality.

In the case of disembodied liberation, the consciousness of personality being lost, the mind also loses its formal existence in *virupa*, or formlessness, whereupon there remains nothing of it.

There remains no more any merit or demerit in it, nor beauty or deformity; it neither shines nor sets any more; nor is there any consciousness of pain or pleasure in it.

It has no sense of light or darkness, nor perception of day and night; it has no knowledge of space and sky, nor of the breadth, height, or depth of the firmament.

Its desires and efforts are lost within its essence, and there remains no trace whatever of its entity or nullity.

It is neither dark nor bright, nor transparent as the sky; it does not twinkle like a star, nor shine forth like the solar and lunar lights. There is nothing to which it may be compared in its transparency.

Those minds that have freed themselves from all worldly cares and passed beyond the bounds of thought, rove in a state of freedom, as the winds wander freely in the region of the air.

Intelligent souls that are serene and still, steadfast in perfect bliss, above the torments of *rajas* and *tamas*, assuming vestures of vacuous form, find their repose in the supreme felicity of union with the Divine.

Upasama Khanda XC

# XII
# VIRAJ

The Sage Vasishtha narrated the discourse of Bhusunda: Just as the supposition is false and wrong, that particular vacuities are parts of or derived from the universal void, so too conception of the supposed ego is altogether an error. This mistaken conception of limited vacuities produced from the unlimited void has given rise to the erroneous belief in ultimately distinct souls proceeding from the one universal and undivided Divine Soul.

Divine Intellect — *Chit* — exists in the form of air as it manifests throughout the aerial sphere, taking air for its vehicle. Similarly, I am neither the ego nor the non-ego. The unity of the subtle conscious Intellect of aerial form contains the gravity of the vast world in itself, just as a ponderous mountain is contained in atoms. The conscious Intellect is of the form of air.

The Intellect itself, rarer than the subtle air, conceives in itself the gross nature of unintelligent matter which it then exhibits as the form of the world. The spiritually wise know that egoism and the materiality of the world are but transformations of Intellect — *vivarta rupa* — just as the currents and swirlings of streams in eddies are but transformations of the water.

With the cessation of this process of intellection — *nivarta rupa* — the entire course of nature is at rest, like the limpid waters of a waveless lake or the quiet sphere of the sky without the stirring agitation of the winds. There is no cause of any physical action in anything or any part or period of the world, except what is derived from the motion of Intellect, without which this whole world is a shapeless void and nullity.

The action of Intellect makes the world appear to us at all places and times, whether as the sky, the waters or as land, and also when we wake, sleep or dream. The action and inaction of Intellect is imperceptible to our understanding owing to the extreme tenuity of the mind, which is more transparent than the crystal sky.

The knowing soul, unified or settled as one with the Supreme Spirit, is unconscious of pleasure, pain or the sense of egoism.

Melted into the divine essence, it resides as the fluidity of the intelligent fluid. The knowing mind has no regard for any external intelligence, fortune, fame or prosperity. Having no desire or hope to rise, nor fear or shame to fall, it sees more of these things before itself, just as no objects of broad daylight are seen in the dark of night.

The moonlight of the Intellect, issuing forth from the moonlike disk of divine glory, fills the universe with its ambrosial fluid. There are no created worlds or receptacles of time and space apart from the essence of Brahman, which fills the whole. The whole universe being filled with the glorious divine essence, it is the Mind that revolves with the spheres of the worlds upon it, like the curling circles upon the surface of the waters.

The revolving world rolls evanescently on, like a stream running to its decay with ever-rising and sinking waves, and its gurgling and whirling eddies and pools. As shifting sands may appear as a lake, and as distant smoke may appear as gathering clouds, so does this world appear to the deluded as a gross object of creation, and a third thing besides Divine Spirit and Mind.

As wood cut by the saw appears as separate blocks, and water divided by the winds appears as detached waves, so does this production within the Supreme Spirit seem to be something without and separate from it. The world is as unsolid and insubstantial as the stem of a plantain tree and as false and frail as the leaves of the arbour of our desire. It is plastic in its form, but as hard as stone in its underlying reality.

It is personified in the form of Viraj, with his thousand heads, feet, arms, faces and eyes, and his body filling every quarter with all the mountains, rivers and realms situated in it. It is void within, and without any pith. Although painted in many colours, it has no colour of itself.

Studded all over with the bodies of *suras* and *asuras, gandharvas, vidyadharas* and great *nagas,* it is inert in itself. It is moved by the all-moving air of *Sutratman* — the all-connecting Divine Spirit — and is quickened by the enlivening breath of the Supreme Soul. As the scene of a great city drawn skilfully upon a canvas appears real to thy sight, so does the picture of the world displayed by imagination on the retina of the mind appear charming to those who do not deign to examine it in its true light.

The reflection of the unreal and imaginary world, falling on the mirror of the fickle and fluctuating mind, appears to swim upon its surface, as a drop of oil floats over the face of water. This world is overspread with the network of the feelings imprinted in the heart, and interspersed with winding eddies of mistake and error. It overflows with the flood of our affections and with the silent murmurs of our sorrows.

The understanding is apt to employ such terms as 'I' and 'thou' as if to things distinct from the original and prime Intellect, but none of these exists apart from the Supreme One, just as fluidity is not other than the water itself. *Chit* — the luminous Intellect itself, is apprehended as the creation. Other than it there is no creation or any creator.

As the power of impulsion is inherent in all moving things, like the blowing of winds or the flowing of waters, so the Intellectual Soul, being devoid of form, knows all things in their void or ideal states only. Just as seas and oceans become the apparent cause of distinct countries by severing the connection of one land to another, though Space remains ever one, so too delusion is the cause of diverse ideas and dreams of material objects, though Spirit remains forever unchangeful.

Know that the words 'mind', 'egoism' and 'understanding', and others significant to the idea of cognition, all proceed from ignorance alone and are soon removed by proper investigation. By conversation with the wise we may remove one-half of this ignorance, and by study of the *Shastras* we may remove another quarter, while our faith in and reliance upon the Supreme Spirit serves to eradicate the remaining quarter altogether.

Having apportioned yourself into this fourfold duty, and destroying by degrees the four parts of ignorance, you will find at last that Nameless One which is the True Reality itself.

Rama said: I understand, O Sage, how a portion of our ignorance is removed by conversation with the wise, so also how a fourth part of it is driven off by study of the *Shastras*, but explain to me how the remainder of it is removed by our faith and reliance in the Spirit. Tell me, Master, what you mean by the simultaneous and gradual removal of ignorance, and what I am to understand by the Nameless One and the True Reality, as distinguished from the unreal.

Vasishtha replied: It is proper for all good and virtuous people, who are dispassionate and disenthralled with the world, to have recourse to wise and holy men and to converse with them regarding the order of nature, for the sake of crossing over the ocean of this world of misery. It is also proper for intelligent persons to be diligent in their search for passionless and unselfish men, wherever they may be found, and particularly to discover and reverence such of them as possess knowledge of the soul and are kindly disposed to impart their Divine Wisdom to others.

Attaining the company of such a holy sage removes half of one's temporal and spiritual ignorance, by setting one on the initial and best step towards Divine Wisdom. Half of one's spiritual gloom being dispelled by association with the Holy, the remaining two-fourths are removed by sacred studies and one's own faith and devotion.

Whenever any craving for any enjoyment whatsoever is carefully suppressed in oneself by one's own endeavour, this is the self-exertion which destroys the fourth part of spiritual ignorance. Thus the society of the Holy, the study of the *Shastras*, and one's own exertion take away one's sins, and this is done by each singly and conjointly, either by degrees or at once.

Whatever remains, either as something or nothing, upon the total extinction of ignorance, the same is said to be the transcendent, nameless and unspeakable. This verily is the real Brahman, the undestroyed, infinite and eternal. This being only a manifestation of immaterial volition, it is also apprehended as the void of Non-Being. Knowing the measureless, immeasurable and unerring BEING, rely upon your own nothingness in *Nirvana*, and be free from all fear and sorrow.

Nirvana Prakarana Purvardha, XII

# XIII
# THE WITNESS

Bhusunda said: This *Kalpa* tree whereon we dwell stands firm and unshaken amidst the revolutions of ages and the all-destroying blasts of tempests and conflagrations.

This great arbour is inaccessible to beings who dwell in other worlds; therefore we reside here in perfect peace and bliss, apart from all disturbance.

When Hiranyaksha, the giant demon of the antediluvian race, strove to hurl this earth with all its seven continents into the lowest abyss, even then did this tree stand firm on its roots at the summit of this mountain.

And then, when this mountainous abode of the gods stood trembling, with all the other mountains of the earth, upon Varaha's tusk, this tree remained unshaken.

When Narayana supported this seat of the gods with two arms, and uplifted the Mandara Mountain with the other two, even then was this tree unmoved.

When the orbs of the sun and moon shook with fear at the terrible warfare of the gods and demons, and the whole earth was plunged in commotion and chaos, still this tree stood firm on its root.

When the mountains were uprooted by hail storms raging with terrific violence, rending away the huge forest trees of this Mount Meru, this tree was unshaken by the blast.

When the Mandara Mountain rolled into the milky ocean and gales of wind filled its caverns, bearing it afloat on the water's surface, and the great masses of diluvian clouds rolled about the vault of heaven, this tree stood steadfast as a rock.

When this Mount Meru was clenched in the grip of Kalanemi, and he was going to crush it by his gigantic might, even then this tree was steady on its root.

When the *Siddhas* were blown away by the flapping wings of Garuda, the king of birds, in their strife to obtain the ambrosia, this tree was unmoved by the wind.

When the serpent which upholds the earth was assailed by Rudra in the form of Garuda, and the world shook from the blast of his wings, this tree was still.

When the flame of the last conflagration threatened to consume the world with all its seas and mountains, making the serpent, which supports the earth on its hoods, throw out living fire from all his many mouths, even then this tree was neither shaken nor burnt down by the awesome and all-devouring fire.

So stable is this tree that there is no danger, O Sage, that can betake us here, just as there is no evil that can betide the inhabitants of heaven. How can we, O Great Sage, ever be exposed to any danger, abiding in this tree which defies all calamities? We are beyond all fears and dangers, like those who dwell in heaven.

Vasishtha asked: Tell me, O Wise One who has borne the blast of dissolution, how you have remained unharmed and undisturbed while many a sun and moon and hosts of stars have fallen and faded away.

Bhusunda replied: When at the end of a *Kalpa* age the order of the world and the laws of nature are broken and dissolved, we are compelled to forsake our abode, like a man departing from his best friend.

We then remain in the air, freed from all mundane conceptions, the members of our bodies becoming devoid of their natural functions, and our minds released from all volitions.

When the zodiacal suns blaze forth in their full vigour, melting down the mountains by their intense heat, I remain with intellect fixed in the Varuna *mantram.*

When the diluvian winds burst with full force, shattering and scattering the huge mountains all around, it is by attending to the Parvati *mantram* that I remain as stable as a rock.

When the earth with its mountains is dissolved into the waters, presenting the face of a universal ocean, it is by the volatile power of the Vayu *mantram* that I bear myself aloft.

I then convey myself beyond this perceptible world and rest in the holy ground of Pure Spirit. I remain as if in profound sleep, unagitated in body or mind.

I abide in this quiescence until the lotus-born Brahmā is again employed in his work of creation, and then I re-enter the confines of the re-created world, where I settle again on this tree.

Vasishtha said: Tell me, O Lord, why other Yogis do not remain as steadfast as you do through your power of *dharana.*

Bhusunda replied: O Venerable One, it is by the inseparable and supreme power of destiny, which none may prevent or set aside, that I live in this way, and others live in theirs.

None may oppose or alter that which must come to pass for them. It is nature's law that all things must be as they are ordained.

It is by the firmness of my intent that things are so fixed and allotted as my share, that they must so come to pass in each *Kalpa* age, again and again, and that this tree must grow on the summit of this mountain and I have my abode in its hollow.

Vasishtha said: Lord, you are as enduring as our salvation is long lasting, and are able to guide us in the paths of truth because established in true wisdom and steady in the intent of *Yoga*.

You, who have seen the many changes of the world and experienced all things through the repeated course of creations, are best able to tell of the wonders to be witnessed during the revolutions of the ages.

Bhusunda replied: I remember, O Great Sage, the earth beneath this Mount Meru to have once been a desolate land, having no hills, rocks, trees, plants, or even grasses upon it.

I remember also this earth under me to have been full of ashes for a period of myriads of centuries of mortal years.

I remember a time when the lord of the day — the sun — was unproduced, and when the orb of the moon was not yet known, and when the earth under me was not divided by day and night but was lighted by the light of this Mount Meru.

I remember this mountain casting the light of its gems upon one side of the valley below, leaving the other in utter darkness, like the Lokaloka Mountain which presents its light and dark sides to people on the two sides of the horizon.

I recall seeing the war between the gods and demons rage high, and the flight and slaughter of people in all the quarters of the earth.

I remember witnessing the revolution of the four *yugas*, and the revolt of the proud and vaunting *asuras*. I have seen the Daitya demons driven back to the wall.

I remember the seed of the earth being borne away beyond the bounds of the universal flood. I recollect the mansion of the world when only the Uncreated Triad remained in it.

I remember seeing no life on earth except for the vegetable

creation through the duration of one-half the four *yuga* ages.

I also recall this earth to have been full of mountains and mountainous tracts for the space of full four *yugas*, when no men peopled the earth and human customs and usages had gained no ground on it.

I remember seeing this earth filled with the bones of dead Daityas and other fossil remains, rising in heaps like mountains, and continuing in their dilapidated and crumbling state for myriads of years.

I remember that formless state of the world when darkness reigned over the face of the deep, when the serpentine support of the earth fled in fear, the celestials left their ethereal courses, and no treetop or bird touched the sky.

I remember the time when the northern and southern divisions of India both lay under the one Himalayan boundary mountain. I recall when the proud Vindhyan Mountain strove to equal great Meru.

These and many other things I remember, which would take too long to relate. But what is the use of long narrations? Attend, and I will tell you the main substance in brief.

I have beheld innumerable *Munis* and *Manvantaras* pass away before me, and I have witnessed hundreds of quadruple *yugas* glide away, one after the other, all filled with great deeds and events, but now buried in oblivion.

I remember the creation of one sole body in this world, named Virat, when the earth was devoid of men and *asuras*.

I remember that age of the world when Brahmins were addicted to wine and drunkenness, when the Sudras were outcasted by the Suras, and when women were involved in polyandry.

I also remember when the surface of the earth presented the sight of one great sheet of water and was entirely devoid of all vegetation, when people were produced without cohabitation of man and woman.

I recall that age when the world was a void and there was no earth or sky nor any of their inhabitants. Neither men nor mountains existed, nor was there sun or moon to divide day and night.

I remember the sphere of heaven shrouded under a sheet of darkness, when there was neither Indra nor king to rule in heaven or earth, and there were no high, low or middle classes of men.

It was after this that Brahmā thought of creating the worlds, and divided them into the spheres of the high, low and intermediate regions. He then established the boundary mountains and distinguished Jambudvipa from the rest.

The earth was not divided then into different nations and provinces, nor were there distinctions of caste, creed or organization for the various orders of its people. There was then no name for the starry frame, nor any denomination for the pole star or its circle.

It was then that the sun and moon had their birth, and the gods Indra and Upendra had their dominions. After this occurred the slaughter of Hiranyakasipu and the restoration of the earth by the great Varaha, the boar *Avatar* of Vishnu.

Then came the establishment of kings over the peoples of the earth and the revelation of the *Vedas* was given to mankind. After this the Mandara Mountain was uprooted from the earth and the ocean was churned by the gods and the giant races of men.

I have seen the unfledged Garuda, the bird of heaven which bore Vishnu on its back; and I have seen the seas breaking up into bays and gulfs. All these events are remembered by me like the latest occurrences in the course of the world. Surely they must be within the memory of my children and of yourself as well.

I have witnessed in former ages Vishnu, with his *vahan* Garuda, become Brahmā with his *vahan* Kalahansa, and witnessed the same transformed into Shiva with the Nandi bull as his bearer.

Nirvana Prakarana Purvardha, XXI

# XIV

# THE YOGA OF SHIVA

Lord Shiva said: This world is composed of reality and unreality and bears throughout the stamp of its origin; it is composed of unity and duality, yet is free from both. The intellect disfigured by dark ignorance views an outer world distinct from an inner. To the clear-sighted there is no separate outer world, but only unity.

The perverted intellect, considering itself the body, is confined therein, but the intellect considering itself a particle of and identical with the divine is liberated from its confinement.

The intellect loses its integrity by dwelling on the duality of its form and sense. Combining with pleasure and pain, it no longer retains its real essence.

Its true nature is free of all denotations and connotations predicated of it. Words pure, undivided, real or unreal, bear no relation to what is an all-pervasive voidness.

Brahmā, the unbounded and inexhaustible, the perfect tranquillity, without second, equal or comparison, expands by its own power like the infinite and empty air, the divine mind stretching in each of the three directions of the three triplicities.

The mind of the Mahatma being untrammelled by its senses and organs, there appears before it a dazzling light. The false world flies away like the shade of night before the sunlight.

The imaginary world falls away like a withered leaf. The living soul remains with its powers of invention and reproduction stilled, like roasted grain.

The intellect, cleared of the cloud of illusion that overhangs the deluded mind, shines like the vault of the autumnal sky, It is termed *pashyanti* from its transcendent vision, and *utsrijanti* from its renunciation of worldly impressions.

The intellect settled in its original, pure repose, gone beyond the commotion of worldly thought, viewing all things in an equal and indifferent light, is said to have crossed over the ocean of the world.

The intellect strong in knowledge of perfect *sushupti* has obtained rest in supreme felicity and is free from the doom of future transmigration.

I have now told you, O Great Vipra, of the curbing and controlling of the mind, the first step in the perfection of the soul by Yoga. Attend to me again concerning the second aspect of the edification and strengthening of the intellect.

This is the unrestricted power of the intellect, perfect in peace and tranquillity, full of light, untinctured by the darkness of ignorance, and broad as the clear vault of heaven.

It is deep as consciousness in profound sleep and hidden as a mark in the heart of a stone. It is delectable as the savour of salt or the scent of wind after a storm.

When the living principle ends its stay in space and time, the intellect flies like an invisible force in the open air, mixing with the transcendent void.

Freed from all thoughts and conceptions, like the calm sea, it becomes as still as the windless air and as imperceptible as the flower in its fragrance.

Liberated from all bondage and ideas of time and space, it is freed from all conception of relation or commonality with the world. Neither subtle nor gross, it becomes a nameless essence.

Unlimited by time and space, it is of the boundless essence of the divine. It is a form and fragment of the quadruple Brahmā-Virat, stainless, pure and undecaying. The far-seeing witness of all things, it is the all in all throughout space and time, self-luminous and far sweeter than any worldly delight.

Such is the second stage of *Yoga* meditation. Attend now, O Sage true to your vows and understanding the process of Yoga, to the third stage.

The vision of Intellect is nameless because, being divine it comprehends all conceptions within its ample sphere, as the great ocean embraces all continents within its expanse. It surpasses the conception of *Brahmatma* in its extent.

By vast and enduring *Kshanti* the soul attains, in the course of time, this steady and unsullied *purushartha* state. It is after passing this and the fourth stage that the soul reaches to its supreme and ultimate felicity.

After passing the successive grades, and until the final state is reached, one must practise *Yoga* in the manner of Shiva, the Mahayogin. Only then will the unremitting holy composure of the third stage be obtained.

Long continuance in this course will lead the pilgrim far, to a state transcending all description, but felt by the holy devotee advancing in his course.

I have already spoken of the stage beyond these three. O Divine Sage, ever remain in that state, if you would attain to the eternal and divine.

This world which seems material will appear infused with Divine Spirit when viewed in its spiritual light, but right observation reveals it to be neither the one nor the other. It is what neither springs into being nor ceases to exist, but is ever calm and quiet, uniform in lustre, swelling and extending like the embryo in the womb.

The non-duality of the divine, and the stillness and solidarity of its intelligence, together with its unchanging nature, prove the eternality of the universe, though it appears instantaneous and evanescent.

The solidity of intellect produces worlds, as the condensation of water produces hailstones, but there is no difference between existence and non-existence, since all things are ever-existent in Divine Mind.

All is Shiva — supreme felicity — quiescence and perfection beyond all description. The syllable OM is the symbol of the whole, and its components comprise the four states of *Yoga*.

Nirvana Prakarana Purvardha, XXXIV

# XV

# MEDITATION UPON SHIVA

Lord Shiva said: Mahadeva is adored by the wise as intellect and conscious soul and also as pervading and supporting all being.

He is situated alike in pots and paintings, in trees and huts, and in the vestures of all men and creatures. He has the several names Shiva, Hara and Hari, Brahmā, Indra, Agni and Yama.

He is both within and without all things, as the Universal Soul, and dwells in the spirit and soul of every wise man. He is worshipped in various forms and modes by diverse peoples.

Hear me first recount, O Great Sage, how this Lord is worshipped as a form and by rituals. Then I shall relate unto you the inward form in which he is worshipped in spirit.

In all forms of worship you must cease thinking of your body, and separate your mind from your personality, however purified it may be. Then you must diligently apply your mind to thinking of pure and bodiless soul which witnesseth the operations of the body from within.

His worship consists solely in inward meditation upon him, and in no outward mode. Apply your mind, in its meditation within your soul, to the adoration of the Universal Soul.

He is of the form of intellect, the source of all light, and is as glorious as millions of suns. He is the light of the inward intellect and is the ground and origin of ego and other, subject and object.

His head and shoulders reach above the Heaven of heavens and his lotus feet descend far below the lowest abyss of space.

His arms extend without bound towards all the directions of space, holding the many worlds of the infinite firmament, wielding them like weapons and armaments.

The worlds rolling over one another rest in the corner of his spacious bosom. His effulgence passes beyond the range of the unlimited void, and his Being surpasses all imaginable bounds.

Above, below, in all four quarters of the compass, He extends exhaustless and endless. He is set about on all sides by hosts of gods, by Brahmā, Rudra, Hari and Indra, as by all the demigods.

All these are but rows of hairs on his body. Their courses of actions are cords binding together the system of the worlds.

His will and destiny are powers proceeding from his Being as active agencies in nature. Such is the Lord, the Mahadeva, always worshipped by the best of men.

He is pure intelligence and the conscious soul, the all-pervading and supporting spirit, present alike in pots and paintings, in all vehicles and all creatures.

He is Shiva, Hari and Hara, Brahmā, Indra and Agni, and also Yama. He is the receptacle of endless beings, the aggregate body of all essences, and the sole entity of all entities.

He contains the mundane sphere, with all its worlds, mountains and other contents. All-powerful Time, which hurls them ever onward, is the guardian at the gateway of his Eternity.

Mahadeva is to be contemplated as residing in some region of this body of eternity and infinity, with this body and its members, and with a thousand eyes and ears.

This figure has a thousand heads and a thousand hands, each holding emblems. It has as many percipient eyes all over its body, and as many listening ears.

It has the powers of touch and taste, as well as hearing, present in all its parts, and that of thinking in its interior mind.

It is, however, beyond all comprehension. It is perfectly good and gracious to all. It is the doer of all things done and the bestower of every blessing.

Situated in the heart of all beings, it is the giver of all strength and energy. Having thought upon the Lord of Lords in this way, the devotee is to acknowledge him in the rituals laid down.

Now hear me tell you, O thou who are best adquainted with Brahmā, the mode of worshipping him in spirit, which consists solely in adoring him in the conscious soul, and not in making ritual offerings.

It requires no fires nor fumigations of incense. It has no need of flowers or decorations, nor does it require oblations of rice, sprinkling of perfumes, or sandal paste.

It needs no exhalation of saffron nor camphor, nor any painting or other thing; nor has it need of any pouring of water.

It is only by the outpouring of the nectar of understanding that he is worshipped. The wise know this as the best meditation and adoration of Deity.

The pure intellect, known to be ever present within oneself, is to be constantly looked into and searched out, heard about and felt, whether one is sleeping, sitting or moving about.

Constantly dwelling on it, and resuming the inquiry quickly if ever left off, one becomes fully conscious of Self, and then should worship the Lord — the self-same Soul — by meditation.

The offering of the heart in meditation unto the Lord is more delectable to him than the sweetest articles of food or the most delicate and fragrant flowers.

Meditation, joined with self-consciousness and contrition, is the *padya* and *arghya* most worthy of the Lord. The best meditation is that accompanied with the flower-self-offering to the Lord.

Without this meditation, it is impossible to realize the Supreme Soul in one's Self. Therefore, spiritual meditation is said to abound with divine grace and the greatest *ananda* and *artha*.

As the animal soul enjoys pleasures in the abode of its body, the rational and spiritual soul derives all happiness in meditation.

The ignorant man who meditates upon Mahadeva for a hundred twinklings of the eye obtains as reward the merit of making the gift of a milch-cow to a Brahman.

The man who worships the Lord in his soul for half an hour in this manner reaps the reward of making the *ashvamedha* sacrifice.

He who meditates upon the Lord in spirit in his own spirit, and presents the offering of his reflections unto him, is entitled to the merit of a thousand such sacrifices.

Whosoever worships the Lord in this manner for a full half-hour receives the reward of making the *raja* sacrifice. By worshipping him in this way at the midday, he obtains the merit of thousands of such sacrifices.

He who worships him in this manner for a whole day settles in the abode of the deity.

This is the superior *Yoga* meditation and the best service of the Lord, as also the highest adoration.

This mode of holy adoration destroys all sins. Whosoever practises it for even a minute with a steady mind is entitled to the veneration of gods and demigods, and is placed in the ranks of emancipated spirits like myself.

Nirvana Prakarana Purvardha XXXVIII

# XVI
# AGNI AND SOMA

The Sage Vasishtha said: Know the world to be a manifestation of the conjunction of intelligence and ignorance, of reality and unreality, among those who have made it thus manifest in themselves and in this form.

The learned call the light of intelligence knowledge, sun and *Agni*, and designate the unrealities of ignorance as dullness, darkness and the coldness of *Soma*.

Rama said: I understand the succession of products of aerial breath and that this air proceeds from *Soma*, but tell me, O Sage, whence comes *Soma* into existence?

Vasishtha replied: *Agni* and *Soma* are mutual causes and effects, being mutually productive and destructive of each other by turns.

Their production is by alternation as that of seed and sprout. Their reiteration is as the returns of day and night. Lasting awhile, they are destroyed instantly, as light succeeds shadow.

When simultaneous, they are seen side by side like sunshine and shade; otherwise, the one is seen with no trace of the other, as daylight and nocturnal gloom are perceived by turns.

There are two modes of causality: that in which the cause is co-existent with its effect, and that wherein the effect comes into appearance after disappearance of its cause.

Causation that is coeval with its effect is termed synchronous, as the seed with its germ, or the tree with its produced seed.

The other is called antecedent causation where the cause disappears before the appearance of its consequent effect, as day results in night, and night in day.

The mode of united cause and effect is exemplified in the instance of the potter and the pot, which co-exist, and being evident to sight needs no further elucidation.

The mode of disjoined cause and effect is exemplified in the succession of day and night which is a sufficient proof of absent antecedent causality.

Those who deny the efficacy of unapparent causes foolishly ignore their common sense, and are themselves to be ignored.

Know, Rama, that an unperceived and absent cause is as evident

70

as any present and palpable cause perceptible to sense. Who would deny that the absence of fire produces cold?

See, Rama, how *Agni* ascends into the air in the form of fumes, which take the shape of clouds in the azure sky, which being again transformed into *Agni* become the immediate cause of *Soma.*

Again, *Agni* being extinghished by cold, it sends its watery particles upward, and this moisture is the antecedent cause of *Soma.*

Submarine *Agni* feeds on the foulness of the seven oceans, and having swallowed their briny waters, disgorges their gases and fumes into the air, flying to the upper sky as clouds that pour pure, sweet waters, like milky drops, into the milky ocean.

Hot Surya devours the frigid sphere of *Soma* in the conjunction of the dark fortnight, and then ejects her in their opposition in the bright half of each month, just as the stork throws off the tender lotus stalk it has taken.

Again, the winds that suck up the heat and moisture of the earth in the spring and summer drop them down as rain in the monsoon, serving to renovate the exhausted body of nature.

Earthly water carried aloft by the sunbeams, called his *karas* or hands, is converted into the solar rays, the immediate cause of *Agni.*

Here water becomes *Agni* by privation of fluidity and frigidity, the antecedent cause of its formation, and by acquisition of dryness and heat, the synchronous cause of transformation into *Agni.*

The absence of *Agni* leaves the presence of *Soma*; the absence of *Soma* leaves the presence of *Agni; Agni* being destroyed, *Soma* takes its place as the departure of day introduces the night.

In the interval of day and night, in the interim between daylight and darkness, and betwixt sunshine and shadow, there is a midmost point and a certain figure in it, unknown to the learned.

That point is no nullity nor empty vacuity, no positive entity, real pivot nor connecting link. It never changes its central place between extremes, or between the states of being and non-being.

By means of the opposite principles of the intelligent soul and inert matter, all things in the universe exist, just as the contraries of light and darkness bring about day and night in succession.

As the course of the world commenced with the union of mind and matter, of mover and moved, so the body of *Soma* was formed by admixture of aqueous and ambrosial particles in the air.

Know, Rama, that the solar beams are composed of ambrosial

particles of *Agni* and that the solar light is the effulgence of intellect, while the mere lunar body is a mass of dull darkness.

The sight of the outward sun in the sky destroys the spreading darkness of night; but the appearance of the intellectual luminary dispels the overspreading gloom of the world from the mind.

Beholding your intellect in the form of the frigid moon, it becomes as dull and cold as that satellite itself, just as the lotus seen at night will not be blooming as in sunshine.

*Agni* in the form of Surya enlightens *Soma* in the same way the light of the intellect illumines the inner body — *lingadeha.* Our consciousness is as the moonlight of the inner soul, and is the product of the sunbeams of our intellect.

The intellect is not engaged in action and is without attribute or appellation; it is like light in the lamp of the soul, and is known in the common light of any lantern that is seen.

The avidity of intellect for knowledge of forms produces the intelligences of the sensible world; its thirst for the inconceivable One brings *Kaivalya,* or its union with that One.

The powers of *Agni* and *Soma* are to be known as united in the body and soul. This union is compared in the *Shastras* to the contact of light and lighted room, or sunshine on a wall.

They are also to be known separately in different bodies and times. Bodies addicted to dullness are actuated by the lunar influence, while persons advancing in spirituality are led on by the solar power.

The warm rising breath is termed *Agni*, while the cool settling breath is termed *Soma.* They abide as light and shade in everyone, ascending and descending and passing from the body.

The cool breath gives rise to warm breath, which remains like the reflection of an object in a mirror. The light of the intellect produces the brightness of consciousness, as the sunbeams reflect themselves like lunar orbs in the dewdrops on lotus leaves at early dawn.

There was a certain consciousness in the beginning of creation with properties of heat and cold, *Agni* and *Soma,* which combined in the formation of the human body and mind.

Strive, O Rama, to settle yourself in that point where *Agni* and *Soma* are in conjunction.

Nirvana Prakarana Purvardha LXXXI

# XVII
# INSTRUCTION OF SHIVA

The Sage Vasishtha said: The Lord crowned with the horn of the moon dwelt on a northern peak of the north polar mountain with his family and attendants.

The mighty but little knowing chief of the Bhringis approached with folded palms and bent low before the divine Lord of Uma.

Bhringi said: Please instruct me, O Lord, for you are the knower of all things, and the Lord of Lords.

I am overwhelmed by sorrow, seeing the raging waves of this deep and dark world in which we are buffeted forever, never finding the calm and quiet harbour of truth.

Tell me, Lord, of that certain truth and inward assurance, on which we may rely with confidence, and whereby we may find both rest and repose in the shattered mansion of this world.

Shiva replied: Always rely on unshaken patience, unmoved by fear or any other cause. Always strive to be foremost in action, enjoyment and renunciation.

Bhringi responded: Explain to me, Lord, who is foremost in action and enjoyment, and what is the greatest renunciation.

The Lord answered: He is foremost in action who performs all deeds whether good or ill, without fear or desire of their fruits.

He who engages in actions, whether good or otherwise, experiencing likes and dislikes, pleasure and pain, but without attachment to any person or thing and without expectation of consequences, is the foremost actor in the theatre of this world.

He acts his part well who acts without ado or anxiety, maintaining a taciturn and pure heart, free of egoism or envy.

He acts his part well who does not trouble his mind with the thought that certain actions are accounted auspicious or inauspicious, righteous or unrighteous, by common opinion.

He performs his part well who is unaffected towards persons and objects, but witnesses all things indifferently, performing his duty without selfish desire or deep attachment.

He is the best actor who is devoid of anxiety and delight, continues in an even tone and tenor of mind, retains constant clarity of understanding, and feels no joy or sorrow at any event.

He performs his duty best whose wits are in readiness at the fittest time for action, but who abides unconcerned at other times, like a reserved and silent sage.

He is foremost in action who performs his works without concern or vain sense of agency, acting his part with his body, but restraining all mental attachment.

He is the best actor who is naturally quiet, never losing an even temper, and engages friends and enemies with an equal heart.

He is the best actor who views birth, life and death, rises and falls, in the same light, never losing mental equilibrium.

He is foremost in enjoyment who neither envies nor pines, and enjoys and accepts his lot with cool composure and poised mind.

He is foremost in enjoyment who receives with his hands what his mind does not perceive, performing bodily action without mental involvement, and enjoys all things with detachment.

He is the greatest enjoyer who witnesses the conduct and behaviour of mankind as an unbiased and unanxious spectator, seeing all without selfish craving.

He whose mind is unmoved by pleasure or pain, and is neither elated with success and gain nor dejected by failure and loss, remaining firm through fierce trials, is the greatest enjoyer.

His enjoyment is best who greets with equal eye decay and demise, danger and difficulty, affluence and poverty, viewing their returns and revolutions with delight and cheerfulness.

He is foremost in enjoyment who sustains the ups and downs of fortune with equal fortitude, as the sea contains its seething waves within its fathomless depth.

He enjoys the highest gratification who is clothed by the virtues of contentment, equanimity and benevolence, as the cooling beams cling to the disc of the moon.

He enjoys himself best who tastes sour and sweet, bitter and pungent, with equal zest, relishing the savoury and unsavoury.

He is always gratified who finds the succulent and tasty equal to the distasteful and dry, and who beholds the pleasant and unpleasant with equal delight.

He to whom salt and sugar are equally palatable, and who remains unaltered in happy and adverse times, is the greatest enjoyer.

He enjoys life best who does not distinguish one food from another or yearn for that which is beyond his right.

He enjoys the highest bliss who braves misfortune with

calmness and brooks his good fortune, his joyous days and better circumstances, with moderation and coolness.

He is foremost in renunciation who has given up all thoughts of his life and death, pleasure and pain, merit and demerit.

He who has abandoned all selfish desires and exertions, forsaken all hopes and fears, and effaced all predispositions from the tablet of his mind, has renounced this world and become free.

He who does not store in his mind pains that invade his body, mind and senses has cast away the troubles of his mortal state.

He is the greatest renouncer who gives up the cares of body and birth and abandons all thought of conventional propriety.

He makes the greatest sacrifice who sacrifices his mind with all its functions and endeavours at the shrine of his self-abnegation.

He who has given up the spectacle of visible things lying before his eye, and does not allow sensible forms to obtrude upon his senses, has relinquished all and everything from himself.

It was in this manner that Lord Mahadeva instructed the chief of the Bhringis, and it is by acting according to these precepts, O Rama, that you must attain to the perfection of Self-regeneration.

Meditate always on the Everlasting Immaculate Spirit, without beginning or end, which is this whole immense universe and is without part or partner, representative or representation. In this way you will become purified and come to be egoless in that self-same Brahmā, the abode of all peace and tranquillity.

Know the one undecaying Brahmā as the soul and seed of all works and productions, the immensity spreading unopened throughout existence, like the endless sky comprehending and manifesting all things in itself.

Know that no thing of positive or potential existence can subsist without or apart from this Universal Essence. Rely securely upon this firm conviction. Be free from all fears in this world.

O most righteous Rama, look always to your inward soul, and perform all outward actions with the outer members of your body, by forsaking the sense of egoism and personality. Being freed from all care and sorrow, you shall attain supreme felicity.

Nirvana Prakarana Purvardha CXV

# XVIII
# RETURNING TO SHIVA

The Sage Vasishtha said: The Goddess dances with her arms outstretched, moving like a swaying forest of tall pines against the empty sky.

She is the power of the intellect, ignorant of herself and ever prone to action, continuing to dance about, bedecked with diverse emblems and devices.

She is arrayed with all kinds of weapons in her thousand arms — the bow and arrow, the spear and lance, the mace and club, the sword, and all sorts of missiles. Conversant with all the elements of being and non-being, she is engaged in every moment of passing time.

She contains the world in the vibration of her mind, as airy cities and palaces are contained in the power of imagination. She herself is that world, as the imagination itself is the utopian city.

She is the volition of Shiva, like the wind in the air. As the air is still without its vibration, so Shiva is quiescent without his volitional power.

This *arupa* volition becomes the *rupa* creation, just as the formless sky produces the wind which vibrates into sound. Thus does the will of Shiva bring forth the world out of itself.

When this volitional energy of Kali dances and plays within the void of the Divine Mind, the world springs forth, as if by union of the active will and the infinite field of that Supreme Mind.

Touched by the dark volitional power, the Supreme Soul of Shiva is dissolved into the waters, just as submarine fire is extinguished by its contact with the waters of the sea.

No sooner does this power come in contact with Shiva, the prime cause of all, than it inclines and turns to assume the veil of nature and its conversion to external forms.

Forsaking her boundless and elemental form, she takes upon herself the gross and limited shapes of land and hills, and then becomes the beautiful forms of forests and flowers.

In the great round she rebecomes the formless void, and again is one with the infinite vacuum of Shiva, just as a river with all its impetuous speed enters into the immensity of the sea.

She becomes as one with Shiva by giving up her identity as an aspect of Shiva. This feminine form of Shiva is merged back into Shiva, the prime male, who is the form of formless void and perfect tranquillity.

Rama asked: Tell me, O Sage, how that sovereign Goddess Shiva could obtain her quietude by coming into contact with the Supreme God Shiva?

Vasishtha replied: Know, Rama, that the Goddess Shiva is the will of the God Shiva. She is styled as nature and famed as the Great Illusion of the world.

The great God is said to be the lord of nature and the prime male. He is of the form of air and is represented as Shiva, calm and quiet as the autumnal sky.

The great Goddess is the energy and will of the Intellect and is ever-active as force in motion. She abides in the world as its nature, and roves about as the great delusion.

She ranges throughout the world as long as she is ignorant of her lord, Shiva, who is ever serenely self-contained, without decay or decrease, beginningless and endless, and without a second.

No sooner is this Goddess conscious of herself as one and the same with the Lord of self-consciousness, than she is joined with her Lord Shiva and becomes one with him.

Nature touching Spirit forsakes her character as gross nature and becomes one with the sole Unity, as a river is absorbed into the sea.

The river falling into the ocean is no more the river but the ocean. Its waters mingling with sea waters become the salt sea.

Just so, the mind cleaving to Shiva is united with him and finds rest therein, as the blade is sharpened by its reduction upon the stone.

The mind engrossed in its own nature forgets the Eternal Spirit and must return again to this world, never attaining spiritual felicity.

An honest man dwells among thieves only so long as he does not know them as such. No sooner does he come to know them than he is sure to shun their company and flee from the spot.

So too the mind dwells among unreal dualities as long as it is ignorant of the transcendent One. But when it becomes aware of True Unity, it is sure to be united with it.

When the ignorant mind comes to know the Supreme Bliss

attendent on the state of *Nirvana*, it is ready to resort to it, as the inland stream runs to join the boundless sea.

The mind roams bewildered in its repeated births in this tumultuous world so long as it does not find its ultimate felicity in the Supreme, unto which it may fly like a bee to its honeycomb.

Who is there that would abandon Divine Wisdom, once having tasted its bliss! Who would forsake the sweet, once having known its flavour. Tell me, Rama, who would not run to sip the delicious nectar which pacifies all our woes and pains, prevents our repeated births and deaths, and puts an end to all our delusions in this darksome world?

Nirvana Prakarana Uttarardha LXXXV

# THE TEN-VERSED HYMN

I am neither earth nor fire, neither air nor ether, neither sensory powers nor all these together, as all of these are transient. I am He that remains alone in deep dreamless rest, the secondless, supreme and attributeless Bliss of Shiva.

I am neither caste nor its divisions, neither rite nor rule, nor am I the fixed mind or mood or mental exercise; this entire illusion of 'I' and 'mine' is rooted in the not-self and is wholly dispelled by the cognition of the Self. I am the secondless, supreme and attributeless Bliss of Shiva.

I am neither mother nor father, neither the gods nor the worlds, neither scriptures nor oblations nor shrines; in deep dreamless rest I am neither abandoned nor in a state of absolute non-existence. I am the secondless, supreme and attributeless Bliss of Shiva.

Neither the Sankhya doctrine nor the Shaiva school, neither the Pancharatra nor the Jaina, neither the Mimamsaka nor any other standpoint, is cognition of *TAT*. Through perfect union, my wholly pure nature is void of all but the Self. I am the secondless, supreme and attributeless Bliss of Shiva.

I am neither above nor below, neither inside nor outside, neither midward nor forward, neither before nor behind; I am indivisible and partless and all-pervading like space. I am the secondless, supreme and attributeless Bliss of Shiva.

I am neither white nor black, neither red nor yellow, neither stooped nor stout, neither short nor tall; I am of the formless nature of self-resplendent consciousness. I am the secondless, supreme and attributeless Bliss of Shiva.

There is neither teacher nor teaching, learner nor learning, neither thou nor I, nor this empirical universe; I am universal self-consciousness, the reality which is untinctured by any modification. I am the secondless, supreme and attributeless Bliss of Shiva.

For me there is neither waking nor dream nor deep sleep, nor am I conditioned by any of these states; all three are of the nature of nescience, but I am the fourth beyond these three. I am the secondless, supreme and attributeless Bliss of Shiva.

All this universe, being other than the SELF, is unreal; the SELF alone is complete, constituting the ultimate refuge, self-established and self-dependent. I am the secondless, supreme and attributeless Bliss of Shiva.

Say not that It is One, as there can be no second, nothing other than That. There is neither uniqueness nor commonality, neither entity nor non-entity; this secondless One is neither void nor plenum. How can I convey this supreme wisdom?

SRI SHANKARACHARYA

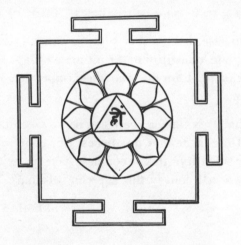

**OM**

# GLOSSARY

| | |
|---|---|
| *Abhichara Vidya* | The art of incantation |
| Agni | The Vedic god of Fire; the oldest and one of the most revered gods |
| *Ahankara* | Conception of 'I'; personality; egotism |
| *Ahanta* | Egoism |
| *Ahavaniya* | The fire of offering; the sacrificial bridge of the Vedas |
| *Ajnana Bhumi* | The seven states of ignorance |
| *Akasha* | The subtle, supersensuous spiritual essence which pervades all space; the primordial substance whose one attribute is sound; the Universal Space in which lies inherent the eternal ideation |
| *Ananda* | Joy, bliss |
| *Arghya* | Libation |
| Arjuna | Disciple of Krishna, instructed by him during the Mahabharatan War |
| *Artha* | Wealth, possessions, worldly goods |
| *Arupa* | Formless |
| *Arupa Manas* | Impersonal Mind; literally, mind without form or qualification |
| *Asansakti* | Worldly indifference |
| *Ashvamedha* | Horse sacrifice; Vedic ceremony performed by kings |
| *Asunya* | Existence |
| *Ativahika* | The everlasting spiritual body |
| *Atmajnani* | Knower of the Supreme Self |
| *Atman* | *Atma*; the Universal Spirit; the seventh and highest principle in man; the Self |
| | |
| *Bhumananda* | The rapture of the earth; the bliss of the world |
| Brahmā | The Creative Logos |
| *Brahman* | The impersonal, incognizable and supreme Principle of the universe; the Absolute; boundless existence; the Supreme Self |
| *Buddhi* | The Universal Soul; the spiritual soul in man (the sixth principle); the vehicle of *Atman*; divine discernment |

| | |
|---|---|
| *Chaitanya Chit* | Cosmic Ideation |
| *Chintamani* | The Jewel of Intellect |
| *Chit* | Abstract Consciousness |
| *Chitti* | The power of intellection |
| *Christos* | The purified, the anointed; he who has united the personal self with the indestructive individuality |
| *Daityas* | Giants, Titans |
| *Dharma* | Sacred Law; duty; righteousness; the Moral Law |
| *Guna* | The three 'threads', qualities or constituents of matter; *sattva, rajas* and *tamas* |
| *Guru* | Spiritual Teacher |
| *Hiranyagarbha* | Radiant or golden egg or womb; the luminous fire-mist or ethereal stuff from which the universe was formed |
| *Ishwara* | The 'Lord' of the universe; the Spirit in man; the eternal Ruler; the controller of *maya* |
| *Jagrat* | The waking state, or a condition of external perception; the first of the states of consciousness |
| *Jiva* | Individual soul |
| *Jivanmukta* | A living embodiment of spiritual enlightenment |
| *Jivatma* | The individual self |
| *Jnana* | Spiritual knowledge or wisdom |
| *Jnana bhumi* | Seven states of knowledge |
| *Jnana Yagna* | Wisdom-Sacrifice |
| Kali | Consort of Shiva; manifestation of the destructive power of Deity |
| *Kalpa* | A cosmic cycle; usually, a 'Day' and a 'Night' of Brahmā, a period of 4,320,000,000 years |

| | |
|---|---|
| *Karana Sharira* | Causal body, corresponding to the principle of *Buddhi* in man |
| *Karma* | Literally, action; the law of ethical causation and moral retribution |
| *Kshanti* | The perfection of patience; calmness |
| *Lingadeha* | Design body; astral vesture |
| Logos | The 'Verbum'; the 'Word'; the manifested Deity, the outward expression of the ever-concealed Cause |
| *Mahajagrat* | Heightened wakefulness |
| *Mahapralaya* | Opposite of *Mahamanvantara*; the total dissolution of the universe |
| *Mahat* | Universal Intelligence, Cosmic Consciousness |
| *Mahatma* | Literally, Great Soul; an exalted exemplar of self-mastery and spiritual enlightenment |
| *Manas* | Literally, the mind; the mental faculty which makes of man a self-conscious, intelligent and responsible individual; the Higher Ego, the reincarnating principle |
| Mandara | Mountain used by the gods to churn the ocean of milk, from which the universe emerged |
| *Manorajyam* | Mental world |
| *Mantra* | Incantation; sacred invocation |
| *Manvantara* | Period of cosmic manifestation, as opposed to *pralaya* |
| Monad | The Unity, the One; the unified triad *(Atma-Buddhi-Manas)*, or the duad *(Atma-Buddhi)*; the immortal part of man |
| Mount Meru | The World-Mountain, variously placed — at the centre of the earth, beyond the Himalayas, the North Pole; the abode of the gods |
| *Muni* | Silent Sage |
| *Naga* | Serpent; serpent-god; symbolically, a wise man |
| *Nimitta* | Instrumental or efficient cause |
| *Nirguna* | Without attributes; *Brahman* |
| *Nirvana* | Complete absorption into the undifferentiated ground of Being; spiritual bliss |

| | |
|---|---|
| *Nivarta rupa* | Negation of intellection |
| *Nischaya* | Without any shadow (of doubt); complete assurance |
| | |
| *Padarthabhava* | Power of penetration into the abstract meanings of things |
| *Padya* | The oblation of washing the feet |
| *Paramatma* | The Supreme Soul of the universe |
| *Pashyanti* | Transcendental vision |
| *Prajnagarbha* | Literally, the womb of unmanifest wisdom; the vesture of enlightenment; self-existence |
| *Pravritti* | Cycle of outgoing; involvement in the process of manifestation |
| | |
| *Raja* | Ruler, sovereign; kingly |
| *Rajas* | The intermediate *guna* pertaining to action and passion |
| Rama | Seventh *avatar* or incarnation of Vishnu; hero of *The Ramayana*; divine king of the golden age |
| *Rishi* | Spiritual Seer; Sage |
| *Rudhadhyasa* | Bias |
| *Rupa* | Literally, form; body or vesture |
| | |
| *Sadhana* | Discipline; practical means to achieve self-transformation |
| *Saguna* | With attributes and all perfections; Brahmā |
| *Samadhi* | Literally, self-possession: the highest state of *yoga*; ecstatic meditation; supreme self-control |
| *Samvid* | Consciousness |
| *Samvritti Swarupa* | Consciousness of one's true nature |
| SAT | Absolute, archetypal Reality; Eternal Truth; absoluteness; self-existence; Be-ness |
| *Sattapatti* | Self-reliance; dependence upon the Divine Spirit as the true refuge of the Soul |
| *Sattva* | The *guna* or aspect of nature whose essence is truth or goodness |
| *Shabda tanmatra* | The essential property of sound |
| *Shastras* | Teachings or sciences; sacred Hindu texts with divine |

| | |
|---|---|
| | or accepted authority |
| Shiva | God belonging to the Hindu Trimurti (Trinity); destroyer of illusions; spiritual regenerator; the patron of *yogins* |
| Shri Shankaracharya | Great philosopher and spiritual Teacher; chief exponent of Vedanta |
| *Siddhas* | Saints or Sages; also a hierarchy of divine beings (Dhyanis) |
| *Soma* | Sacred ambrosia; elixir of immortality; symbol of secret wisdom |
| *Sthula deha* | The physical body or mortal vesture |
| *Subhechha* | Desire for goodness |
| *Suddha Chit* | Pure Intellect |
| *Suddha Sanmatra* | Pure Being |
| *Sukshma Sharira* | The dreamlike illusive inner body; similar to the 'thought-body' |
| *Sunya* | Voidness, absence of manifestation |
| *Suras* | Gods, *devas* |
| *Sushupti* | Deep, dreamless sleep |
| *Sutratman* | Literally, the thread of the Spirit; the immortal individuality |
| *Swapna* | Dreamy consciousness |
| *Swarupa* | One's true form |
| | |
| *Tamas* | The *guna* or aspect of nature whose essence is darkness |
| *Tanmatras* | Rudiments of the five elements; earth, water, fire, air and ether; the subtle essence of these |
| *Tanumanasa* | Subduing the mind; mental restraint |
| TAT | Literally, That; *Brahman*; beyond the three worlds; the pre-existent |
| *Tattvajnani* | Knower of all essences |
| *Turiya* | Literally, the fourth; state of consciousness, corresponding to *samadhi*; spiritual wakefulness |
| *Turiyagati* | Knowledge of Deity; universalization; attainment of spiritual wakefulness |
| | |
| *Utsrijanti* | Renunciation of worldly impressions |

| | |
|---|---|
| *Vahan* | Vehicle |
| Vasishtha | Vedic sage; Teacher of Rama; one of the seven great Rishis |
| *Vicharana* | Discretion |
| *Vidyadharas* | Male and female deities; possessors of knowledge |
| *Vijajagrat* | Embryonic waking |
| Viraj | The Logos; the male Manu created in the female portion of Brahmā's body *(Vach)* |
| *Virinchi* | Volitional soul |
| Vishnu | God belonging to the Hindu Trimurti (Trinity); the preserver; all-pervading solar energy (from *vish*, 'to pervade'); infinite space |
| *Vivarta* | Source |
| *Vivarta Rupa* | Transformations of Intellect |
| | |
| *Yoga* | Spiritual discipline; union with the divine |
| *Yuga* | Thousandth part of a *kalpa*; an age or cosmic epoch |

# CONCORD GROVE PRESS

# SANGAM TEXTS

# SACRED TEXTS

THE DIAMOND SUTRA (with selections from Buddhist literature)

RETURN TO SHIVA (from the *Yoga Vasishtha Maharamayana*)

THE GATHAS OF ZARATHUSTRA (Zoroastrian texts)

TAO TE CHING by Lao Tzu

THE GOLDEN VERSES OF PYTHAGORAS
    (with the commentary of Hierocles)

IN THE BEGINNING (from the *Zohar*)

THE GOSPEL ACCORDING TO THOMAS

THE SEALS OF WISDOM (from the *Fusus al-Hikam*) by Ibn al-ʿArabi

# INSTITUTE OF WORLD CULTURE

NOVUS ORDO SECLORUM by Raghavan Iyer

THE SOCIETY OF THE FUTURE by Raghavan Iyer

THE BANQUET (Percy Bysshe Shelley's translation of Plato's *Symposium*)

THE DREAM OF RAVAN *A Mystery*

THE RELIGION OF SOLIDARITY by Edward Bellamy

THE LAW OF VIOLENCE AND THE LAW OF LOVE by Leo Tolstoy

OBJECTIVITY AND CONSCIOUSNESS by Robert Rein'l

THE DWARF AND THE GIANT by Pico Iyer

The CGP emblem identifies this book as a production of
Concord Grove Press, publishers since 1975 of books and
pamphlets of enduring value in a format based upon the Golden
Ratio. This volume was typeset in Journal Roman Bold, and
Bodoni Bold, printed and softbound by Sangam Printers. A list
of publications can be obtained from Concord Grove Press,
P.O. Box 959, Santa Barbara, California 93102, U.S.A.